Goddess Style
Weight Loss

Wiccans – Happy, Healthy and Confident

from GoddessHasYourBack.com

Moonwater SilverClaw

Wiccan High Priestess
Blogger/Founder of
GoddessHasYourBack.com

with visitors from **178 countries**

A QuickBreakthrough Publishing Edition

More copies are available from the publisher with the imprint QuickBreakthrough Publishing. For more information about this book contact: askawitchnow@gmail.com

This book was developed and written with care. Names and details were modified to respect privacy.

Other Books by Moonwater SilverClaw:

- Goddess Has Your Back
- Goddess Walks Beside You
- The Hidden Children of the Goddess
- Be a Wiccan Badass
- Beyond the Law of Attraction to Real Magick
- Goddess Reveals Your Enchanted Light

Praise for Moonwater SilverClaw:

• "Moonwater was telling me about her **weight loss program** and it sounded like something I could do that didn't cost me more than the normal groceries I buy, anyway. I started with an egg omelet in the morning with mushrooms and spinach. ... In two weeks, I lost 7 lbs. I had a couple of days of eating what I wanted but not overeating. Then right back to *Goddess Style*. I feel great and eat what the Goddess gives us." – Denise Kopplinger

• "In her book *The Hidden Children of the Goddess*, Moonwater brings Wicca to life, enveloping you in the mystery and magick of the Craft. Her writing talent is amazing! Her kindness and even sense of fun is ever present throughout her writing. Moonwater expresses profound Wicca concepts through examples in her own life experience. Wicca actually saved her life. and empowered her to leave an abusive marriage, and this shows the power of this sacred path to positively change the course of our lives, too. Moonwater's stories personally inspire me, and I am confident that they will inspire you also." – Rev. Patrick McCollum, internationally recognized spiritual leader working for human rights, social justice, and equality; the 2010 recipient of the Mahatma Gandhi Award for the Advancement of Pluralism.

• "Religion scholars in the future will likely view Moonwater SilverClaw as the pivotal voice that helped change the discourse on Wicca. In her book *Goddess Has Your Back,* Moonwater reveals Wicca as a very positive and ultimately uplifting spirituality choice. She demystifies the religion's taboos and spooky stereotypes through her unintimidating presentation that clarifies the topic. She introduces the Goddess and the magick rituals that, when used properly, can positively impact your everyday life. The author relays her very personal perspective on the subject and shows how to integrate the philosophies and practices of the centuries-old religion. Looking for a fresh perspective on spiritual growth? Read what Moonwater SilverClaw has to say." – Stacy D. Horn

• "Moonwater's writing will give you a portrait of a woman who lives her faith, and whose life was saved by it. Because so many lives, my own included, were irrevocably changed by Wicca, were given new focus, new purpose, and perhaps most importantly, new personal power to realize one's dreams and ambitions.... It's a story about making your own happy endings, about rescuing yourself...." – Jason Pitzl-Waters, former blogger at WildHunt.org

Visit Moonwater's blog: www.GoddessHasYourBack.com

CONTENTS*

These are highlights. There is much more material in this book!

DEDICATION AND ACKNOWLEDGEMENTS

This book is dedicated to the God and Goddess. Thanks to Tom Marcoux for editing. Thanks to Kay Pannell for her guidance and friendship.

Thank you and blessings to you, the reader.

GoddessHasYourBack.com

For insights about spells, rituals, and more
**Visit GoddessHasYourBack.com
for blog posts and to sign up for
Moonwater SilverClaw's E-newsletter.**

Goddess Style Weight Loss

What if you could invite Goddess to help you lose weight?

Imagine:

You'll learn a system of weight loss that is *not* a diet, and you'll be honoring the God and Goddess through the practice of Wicca.

You'll take care of yourself.

You will *not* be hurting yourself with denial of your favorite foods all the time.

You'll even be nurturing yourself and feeling the embrace of the Goddess.

This book is about being healthy. It's *not* about being stereotypically attractive like any image portrayed in the media.

In fact, Wiccans appreciate Goddess in Her *many* forms.

I'll put this in few words. I have permanently dropped 36.8 pounds. I didn't do it to please my husband. I didn't do it to please society. I did it for me.

You might ask is 36.8 pounds important? My health is

better. I do take care because I see how my mother deals with diabetes.

My intention is to keep exercising and making healthy eating choices.

Along the way, I realized that I had taken on a process which I now call *Goddess Style Weight Loss*.

This book is about how to improve your health and weight through honoring the Gods, the environment and yourself.

Over and over again, I hear about women who were attacked in their younger years, and they did something to get "bigger" or at least, to "be unattractive to male attention."

My first husband was abusive. Through Wicca, I gained the strength to leave him! For me, Wicca has been a life-saver. And now, Wicca—in terms of Goddess Style Weight Loss—is my path of getting physically healthier.

Weight loss is a part of our journey. The problem is that many of us have developed weight troubles *in response to traumas in our lives.*

Author Roxane Gay was gang-raped when she was 12 years old. She writes in her book, *Hunger: A Memoir of (My) Body,* "I ate and ate and ate in the hopes that if I made myself big, my body would be safe. I buried the girl I was because she ran into all kinds of trouble. I tried to erase every memory of her, but she is still there, somewhere. . . . I was trapped in my body, one that I barely recognized or understood, but at least I was safe."

Perhaps, you relate in some way to getting heavy due to wanting to be safe! Some of us have become heavy so we could "disappear" and get away from male attention.

I have dropped 36.8 pounds. I've kept them off. Bringing

my Wiccan faith into the mix has helped.

Sure, I make certain to cast Circle and to gather with my coven.

I often do a candle-lighting ritual. (I certainly light a candle to say 'thank you!' to Goddess Squat for parking spaces!)

But I've brought a *Goddess Style* to my eating habits now. I'm on purpose with eating that which comes from the Goddess and dropping processed "food."

Every day, I eat natural plants (unprocessed) and natural animal protein (unprocessed).

The big change is that I keep processed sugar and carbs out of my diet as much as I can.

Here's my point: These changes have helped me in two ways: I get closer to my Gods and move forward with my healthy goal of weight loss.

I'm grateful to God and Goddess for Their Support.

I've learned that as I take better care of myself and I connect with God and Goddess, **I do NOT need the extra weight to feel safe.**

After all the neglect and physical abuse in my childhood … I can now be free.

What if I chose *(on the spiritual plane before this incarnation)* that I was going to take a journey in which I'd be hurt deeply, long for safety and then rise up to have a new goal … to … be … FREE.

Is that what you want, my friend? To be free?

This book *not* the standard fare. This is *not* a diet book. We're talking about a refreshing, empowering lifestyle: *Goddess Style.*

Here are Sections of this Book:

1. Connect with God and Goddess
2. Goddess Style Interactions with Food
3. Release Yourself from the Need for Extra Weight to Feel Safe
4. Be Smart about Having Energy
5. Create Lots of Self-Care and Comfort (so food fades into the background)
6. Protect Yourself
7. Be Smart about Keeping Yourself Strong and Free of Energy-Drainers
8. Attract Something You Want
9. Create Abundance and Your Own Confidence

Let's get started.

Section One
Connect with God and Goddess

We begin with God and Goddess because that's exactly why this process is *different*.

How's that? We draw on God and Goddess's strength to help us in our new choice of *Goddess Style Weight Loss*. Connecting with your own personal God and Goddess is the first step.

Section One:
Connect with God and Goddess #1

How a Wiccan Makes a First Connection to a God or Goddess Who Is a Great Match

One of my readers of my blog GoddessHasYourBack.com asked, "How do you find a God or Goddess you can have a deep connection with?"

The best way I can answer this is to share with you the journey of two people: Rhonda and Jerry.

Rhonda found her experience to be one of intuition and simply flowing into the presence of the Goddess Hecate (known as the Greek Goddess associated with witchcraft and prosperity).

Rhonda wanted prosperity to flow into her life. At a bookstore, she reached for a book on Wicca. Rhonda was surprised when the book opened to a page that informed her of Hecate.

On the other hand, Jerry went on a conscious quest to find a God to connect with. He studied various pantheons and saw which pantheon interested him. He found that Nordic Gods have a certain fascination for him. Jerry took special care to study what Odin finds to be suitable offerings. Under the guidance of an elder, Mark, Jerry cast a Circle and made an appropriate offering to Odin.

(**Warning:** Make sure to cast a Circle. Make an offering or call out to a God or Goddess from the safety of a Circle. Why? Because when you reach out to another spiritual plane, you do not know if you may attract some entity that can cause you trouble. The Circle is your safety precaution. Additionally, be specific when you call out for a particular God or Goddess.)

In summary: Whether your God/Goddess finds you, or you take a journey to find Him or Her, we, Wiccans, discover various ways to connect with a patron God or Goddess.

Section One:
Connect with God and Goddess #2

Goddess's Point of View about ...
When You Dread Getting on Weight Scale

Just imagine. What does Goddess think as you approach your weight scale? Will She judge you?

Still, if you dread getting on the weight scale, I'm with you.

There have been times when I've dreaded getting on the scale because I had faltered on some days. I ate more than I planned. And I ate the bad stuff.

Now I only get on the scale *once a week*. I tell myself, "It's just information. It's not about using a judgment device."

Where do the judgments come from? Not the scale. If you're like me, the judgment can rise from your own desire to be "perfect" and to do your weight loss process "perfectly."

Not possible. We're human beings. The God and Goddess love us and know we are doing our best. If there were too many "oops days," you will get feedback. Okay. It's feedback that you can use to guide you to do better in the new week. That's the big shift in thoughts. Aim to "do better." Stop falling into the trap of "trying to be good."

You ARE a good person who is working with your weight loss process.

Section One:
Connect with God and Goddess #3

Crying Out to Goddess and God When You Feel Emotionally Overwhelmed

When I am feeling overwhelmed, I ask the God and Goddess for help. Let's face it, They have more resources than I do to figure things out. They have a different perspective and give good counsel when asked.

How do you access Goddess' counsel? I find that meditation offers an opportunity to connect with Goddess.

Sometimes, I steal a quiet moment and ask: "Oh, Lord and Lady, give me strength to keep me on my path."

Later, I will light a candle and ask the same.

We can envision the candle's light as Their love for us.

Making a Shift to a New Pattern When We're Emotionally Overwhelmed

Talk with a thin person and ask, "What do you do when you're emotionally overwhelmed?"

"I go for a walk," Marina says.

"I get on my home treadmill," Janet says.

We notice that they focus on getting in motion.

My heavier friends have this reply: "I eat."

We can notice a significant difference in how thin people and heavy people burn off their uncomfortable emotions.

Is food your refuge?

Is that ultimately breaking down your health?

Then, it's time to instill a new pattern for your ways of dealing with feeling emotionally overwhelmed.

First, "call out" that you're feeling emotionally overwhelmed.

Second, ask the God and Goddess for help.

Third, listen for quiet urgings from your intuition (informed by God and Goddess).

Perhaps, you get the guidance: "Go for a walk."

Do *not* hesitate. Grab your coat and step outside.

If possible, get in motion within five seconds. Why? A number of researchers and authors have noted that if we don't take immediate action, we're likely to be talked out of doing anything. How? Have you thought, "Oh, I'm just too tired to walk"? Then what happened? Nothing. Right? You didn't go for the walk on numerous occasions. (True?)

Instead, counter that with: "Yeah, I'm tired. I'll take my tired butt and walk half a block out and half a block back."

Perhaps, you'll walk further. Or at least, you'll burn up some calories *and* increase your capacity for exercise.

Author Jill Konrath notes she does much of her best thinking while walking. Even better, she feels refreshed when she returns to her work desk.

Again, I invite you to note your feeling overwhelmed and go direct to the Source of comfort—the God and Goddess.

Section One:
Connect with God and Goddess #4

A Goddess Viewpoint about *Going to Bed Earlier*

Wiccans revel in the knowledge of the seasons. At certain times, we notice how the Goddess more expansively demonstrates her beauty and bounty. The Goddess in springtime is fertile, and She holds great promise for more and better.

Wiccans also note that the seasons, in a way, appear in *one day.*

We observe dawn, high noon, and dusk.

Midnight is the cold of winter.

Dusk and dawn represent the equinoxes

High noon appears like summer.

I'll take this another step. The God runs out of energy in the winter until He dies (really, He leaves for the underworld where He recharges).

This brings me to Goddess Style Weight Loss.

15

How would Goddess advise us to use our day and choose when to sleep?

Many of us, like the God, start to "fade out" at the end of the day. When it is getting late in the evening, I eat more of the wrong things to stay awake. To me, nibbling at night is a good indicator that it's time to go to bed.

I can take a moment and realize, I'm like the God in winter. My clock is running down. I really need to go to where I can recharge. (The God can keep the underworld. I belong in bed.)

In my house, family members have cookies and more on the first floor. My solution is to "run away, run away" up the stairs away from the first floor.

Do you need to set your alarm and start your "going to sleep ritual" earlier at night?

Do you need to stay away from the kitchen, or dining room table? Do you need to store all processed foods (like cookies) in cupboards?

Do you simply need to get your body into bed sooner?

Remember, Goddess loves it when you're healthy and happy. Get thee to bed.

Section One:
Connect with God and Goddess #5

Keep Your Sense of Humor

My editor said, "When have you been funny?"
"Funny looking or funny smelling," I quipped.
Then I said, "We're really reaching low in the bag here."
That's when he burst out laughing.

Think about it. Where does a lot of humor arise? From low points. We, who struggle with our weight, face low points, just about every week.

When I talk about keeping a sense of humor, I want to make an important point. When talking *to other people*, do NOT put yourself down.

I repeat, *Do NOT put yourself down.*

My friend, Tabby, said, "Without self-defecating humor I'd have no humor at all!"

That wasn't a typo. That's Tabby's sense of humor. She

replaced the usual word, *self-deprecation.*

All humor has a target.

I invite you to make the most of humor-moments during the day.

I suggest that you to pick safer targets like: "That cupcake, kicked me in the shin and jumped in my mouth."

Recently, I had a conversation about humor with my husband. He noted that humor is about:

- Exaggeration
- A sudden twist
- The punch word at the end of the sentence.

If you don't seem to have a way with words, still consider watching something funny each day: a TV show or funny videos on YouTube. (Oh, cats, you're not as smart as you think you are ...)

Laughter reduces the effects of stress by increasing the body's production of serotonin and endorphins. A natural high. And it's free ... unlike other things ...

Keeping a Sense of Humor by Taking Yourself Lightly

It's a classic idea that we would do better to NOT take ourselves so seriously.

First, make sure you're getting enough sleep because the world looks *dimmer* through sleep-deprived eyes.

It begins with your metaphor about life.

I like to say that *life is a classroom.*

Other people say, "Life is a bitch, and then it has puppies."

My point is: If you expect life to be awful—guess what?—that's what you get.

Instead, with a whimsical smile, just shrug your shoulders and say, "Oops. There I go again."

Then dust yourself off. Carry on.

Section One:
Connect with God and Goddess #6

Avoid "Denial" and Food Becoming Too Important in Your Life

Do you have a favorite food that is loaded with processed sugar?

I do. Ice cream, cake, donuts, pastries, pizza, milkshakes …

You get the idea.

The focus of Goddess Style Weight Loss is to *avoid* having an obsession and saying that "we must deny ourselves."

Goddess Style is just that—a new lifestyle.

If you deny yourself of a favorite food for a long period, you might cause yourself more hurt than necessary. It is likely that it is better to make a good choice about having a bit of that favorite food on occasion.

Denying all pleasurable foods is like denying *the shadow side* of our being.

The Shadow Side includes fears, hate, anger,

uncomfortable desires and other things that we deny.

Just because we do not see the sun at night does not mean it winked out of existence. The same reality is about our Shadow Side. What many people experience is: "Deny your Shadow Side and then it makes itself felt—explosively."

Such denial is *not* a skillful way to approach living in a healthy manner.

I've seen that people who say, "I'm only *white light*" then, later, they explode like a volcano that devastates the country side.

So, let's avoid you "exploding."

Skillfully choose when and how to have a small portion of your favorite food. (Then food does *not* become too important in your life.)

Life is *not* just meant to be endured. Life is an adventure with pitstops that can, on occasion, include favorite foods with … wait for it … processed ingredients.

Moderation, people!

I've noticed that being too strict can set many of us up to fail.

Make your choices. Own your choices.

For example, just last night, my husband and I celebrated our completion of creating an online course. (That was a lot of work!)

So, I chose to have an amazing chocolate cupcake, topped with …

I'll stop here.

I had the treat last night. No need to get my "chocolate-desire engine" started now!

And I decided to skip chocolate cupcakes, at least, for the next week.

It's about making good choices.

Section Two
Goddess Style Interactions with Food

How do you interact with your food?

Do you use it as a way of escape, comfort, or something else? Why and what do you eat?

How much do you eat in each sitting? These are questions you need to ask yourself while in the process of *Goddess Style Weight Loss.*

Many of us find life's past traumas play a significant role in how, what and why we eat. Where is the healthy and happy in your relationship with food?

This **lifestyle** requires you to rethink your relationship with food.

Section Two:
Goddess Style Interactions with Food #1

Wiccans and "Goddess Style" for Health and Happiness

"I'm tired of people saying that being fat is about putting a barrier up to protect yourself," my friend, Rhonda, said.

"Do you think that it's not true?" I asked.

"No. I'm just tired of it," she said, with a weak little smile.

When I was a child, I was beaten by my brother. I got married too young to an abusive guy.

Are you getting the pattern?

(By the way, through being empowered by Wicca, I divorced that guy.)

We, who have had such experiences, don't feel safe and so we eat—not just for comfort. Some of us eat and get fat so we can just avoid the whole situation of being sexually attractive. If you've been violated, doesn't it make sense to take yourself out of a threatening situation. At a certain point with weight gain, predatory male individuals do not pay attention to you. It's almost like disappearing.

Sometimes, we even feel like we don't deserve to be happy. Think of how much shaming the mainstream media (including entertainment TV shows) does toward plus-size people.

Much of my weight problems stemmed from such low feelings (even though I would have said, "No. I don't have those issues. I just want to eat what I want to eat.")

With my experiences as a child and teen, I felt scared, vulnerable, unloved, and unworthy. Eating was the comfort I found. And I ate, and I ate, bringing me up to an unhealthy 278 lbs.

So, I suggest that for some of us eating is a psychological issue. It's not just about willpower. In fact, relying on willpower is NOT a good plan.

Finally, I've worked with a doctor who brought an important detail to my attention: "Drop the carbs and the processed sugar," he said.

I am glad to say that I've trimmed down 36.8 lbs. from the 278 lbs. I once was.

Weight Loss as a Spiritual Journey

I realize that my losing the weight also has a spiritual component. Just recently, I noticed that I had two "oops days" (eating too much and processed sugar) in a row. My sweetheart asked me, "So two oops days? Are you upside down?"

The answer was *yes.* I had been enduring lots of stress, and I felt disconnected from my spiritual essence. That's the part of me that IS really safe no matter what tough moments arise in my regular life.

When You're in Trouble About Your Eating Habits ...

To get to a form of inner peace, I lit a candle and said, "God and Goddess, please give me the strength to continue on my path of Healthy Eating."

Taking in the Goddess—The "Goddess Style" of Healthy Eating

I call my new way of healthy eating "Goddess Style." It's about only eating what comes from the ground or a womb. No processed foods. No carbs and no sugar. Since most carbs are processed in some way, we avoid pasta, bread, and tortillas. We even avoid beans and rice (they're still carbs).

You see, I eat only fresh veggies and unprocessed meats like whole breast chicken and so forth. I do eat cheese. (Yum!)

When you eat from the ground and the womb you are honoring the Gods. You are taking in the sustenance straight from Mother Earth. She provides real nourishment for our bodies and souls.

Some People Like "Advanced Goddess Style"

My friend, Nadine, is a vegan. Why? She says, "Eating abused animals brings on bad karmic energy." Sometimes, I think of the vegan-choice as "Advanced Goddess Style."

I also realize that plants can be tainted by pesticides. Try to eat local and organic if you can. Or even better, if you have the space, grow some food in your own garden. In this way, you will know for sure where your food has come from. You can use Google to find articles about growing fruits and vegetables indoors.

In summary, when we take in "purely natural foods," both our body and soul receive great nourishment. You might say that such natural foods also enhance our soul with good karma. The God and Goddess are in everything around us: The food we eat, and the world around us. When we take in natural foods, it is taking the essences of the Gods into ourselves. Undiluted, unfiltered, natural and healthy.

It pleases the Gods when we honor them with a natural lifestyle, what I call the Goddess Style of living. Our bodies work better, and we feel better.

If you choose to go Goddess Style, you will be healthier and happier.

Section Two:
Goddess Style Interactions with Food #2

Healthy Eating—Goddess Style

Would you like to drop some excess weight? I'm glad to share with you that I've let go of 36.8 lbs. so far. "How?!"—my friends ask.

At my blog GoddessHasYourBack.com, I sometimes write about my new lifestyle that includes no carbs and no sugar (except for the occasional "oops day.") I'm now calling this new lifestyle: Goddess Style. You'll notice that I don't use the word "diet."

Why do I say Goddess Style? Because everything I eat comes from the Goddess. I only eat stuff from the ground or from the womb, which the Goddess oversees. What can be more Pagan than that? (The opposite is shoving processed foods into ourselves, clogging arteries and doing damage.)

Now, we'll add a Food Prayer.

Food Prayer

I thank You Goddess and God for the nourishment I am about to consume.
May it provide health and strength unto my body.
May it brighten my spirit with newfound wisdom.
May it bring joy to my heart.
By the Lord and Lady, blessed be this food.
So mote it be.

May you find some comfort from these ideas.

Special Note about What I Eat:

Do **NOT** start any kind of diet without a doctor's supervision.

People have asked me what I'm doing and I reply that I started my change in eating habits **with a doctor's learned advice.**

My food habits include eating fresh vegetables—raw or cooked.

I eat unprocessed protein which includes salmon, steak, and chicken.

My doctor advised that I avoid carbohydrates to a great extent. So, I avoid grains (in general), beans, oatmeal, breads, rice, potatoes, pasta, cake, donuts and other pastries.

You might be surprised of what I do eat: sour cream, cheese, guacamole, carrots, and fruit (except bananas).

Section Two:
Goddess Style Interactions with Food #3

Wiccan Way to Better Health

Would you like to drop excess weight? I'm on this path now.

At my blog GoddessHasYourBack.com, I wrote about my *great results in four weeks:*

"I'm grateful to say that I have lost [at that time] at least **11.4 pounds in four weeks.** What's my secret?

I'm approaching this process with Wicca helping me all the way. I have magick on my side. This is a great start.

Additionally, the other secret weapons are my diet and my walking. During my experience thus far, I'm not even hungry.

"What's she eating?" you might ask.

Veggies and protein. Lots of veggies. No sugar and no carbs. That's no bread, pasta, tortillas, rice or beans. It sounds rough, but it's really not. How?

I can eat bacon and still lose weight. Yum! I can have

cheese and other things that you would normally not think of as "diet" food.

How is this a Wiccan way? I eat only things that come out the ground or from a womb. Just as nature intended. I stick to the foods of the earth. Yes, I know wheat is from the ground, but it is usually processed into bread and other things. I just stay away from carbs. Usually carbs are processed. I am eating things that have not been processed, and that's the key.

For example, for breakfast I can have an apple and peanut butter (only peanuts with salt—no sugar that is found in a leading brand) with stir-fried veggies.

Tip: Use the bacon grease for the oil to fry the veggies. This makes them bacon flavored! (As with all diet plans and exercise plans, be sure to check with your doctor before starting any kind of restrictive diet. For example, if you have cholesterol problems, you may want to skip the bacon.)

I am eating the treasures of the earth and losing weight. I eat eggs, chicken and fish. My diet is now mostly vegetables. When possible, I like to eat vegetables from local suppliers. This helps with the sustainability of the planet.

I like helping Mother Earth and losing weight at the same time!

How about you?

Section Two:
Goddess Style Interactions with Food #4

About Backsliding and Trying to Calculate a Way Get What You Want

"Is Goddess Style Weight Loss some form of diet?" my friend, Glenn, asked.

"No!" I said, with vigor.

Goddess Style Weight Loss is a spiritual process. It *does* involve choosing to eat natural food directly from the Goddess. We choose to avoid as much processed food, including processed sugar, as possible.

Still, there are times when chips are just too tempting and that cookie is just asking for it!

Backsliding happens.

Be kind to yourself. The God and Goddess love you, so how about you love yourself?

Things happen. In May, I did some backsliding. I went camping for a week, and there were two birthdays in my family that month. It is hard to stay in the woods without eating beans and other carbs. Sugar abounded as well.

When I returned, it was two birthdays with dinners in restaurants and …. CAKE!

When the cake hits the fan, it is good to keep your sense of humor.

Trying to Calculate a Way Get What You Want

Have you found yourself trying to somehow make a food choice to sound "okay" to yourself? It sounds like: "Oh yeah, cake for breakfast. It has dairy products in it!"

I invite us to take a moment and face reality. We say *"okay."* It sounds like: *"Okay. I do not* want a life without chocolate chip cookies. I'll just make a *new choice.* Instead of a bag of cookies, I can choose to go to the grocery store and buy one cookie at the bakery. They'll hold onto the extra cookies for me. And I'll make a special trip to get my glorious cookie for the month."

This may sound extreme. But you do succeed in keeping the cookies out of your home.

Goddess Style is NOT a Diet; It's a Lifestyle

Remember this is a *Lifestyle.* It's the way you now live from this point on. It's the choices we make that create who we are.

Sometimes, your choice is to nurture yourself and to keep a variety of things in your life. Having cake two times in one particular month is not a terrible tragedy.

Maybe, you'll want to just take two bites next time.

I've noticed that many people I know who seek to lose weight make a mistake (oops, had a second slice of pizza!) into a tragedy.

I just call it a mistake. Then I say to myself, "I'll do better. The Gods know it's just a mistake."

We can use a mistake as a stepping stone.

Section Two:
Goddess Style Interactions with Food #5

A Goddess's Viewpoint of "Oops Days" and "Conscious Choice Days"

My editor for this book asked, "Are you going to include 'Cheat Days'?"

"I don't relate to that. Who are you cheating on?" I said.

Later, he asked, "How about 'Pre-selected Release Days'?" By this, he explained that he wanted to know how and when we might "give ourselves a break."

I thought about it.

I'm concerned about two things, First, it does you no good to beat yourself up for an occasional misstep when you might have a piece of pie, although you're committed to avoiding processed sugar.

Second, the idea of a "cheat day" just bugs me. It makes me feel like I am cheating myself and the Gods for not following through on my commitment.

Does this seem true to you?

Here's the thing. It's okay to take one moment or even a day to celebrate with friends. You can have a piece of cake with your Mom to celebrate her birthday. Don't feel guilty. We are *human*. The Gods know this. They love us and want to see us succeed. They are *not* drill sergeants who demand you do everything perfectly.

But make sure it is *ONE* day, **not** two, **not** three or more days. This One Day is something I call a "Conscious Choice Day." For example, my husband recently asked: "For our anniversary, do you want to go out and have dessert?" I said, "Yes!" Once a year, I certainly want to celebrate our anniversary with dessert.

So, when it comes to either a "Conscious Choice Day" or an Oops Day, remember, we are in this for the long haul. It's a total lifestyle change. Be kind to yourself when first starting. You will have oops moments. Just acknowledge them and think about why you ate what you ate. If your answer is *I simply wanted to because I was sad*, then address it.

It is important to recognize oops days. Remember our goal is to connect with God, Goddess, and the world around us naturally. Let's *not* torture ourselves. So, if you eat something processed, don't beat yourself up about it. Just acknowledge it, meditate on why you ate it and continue onward with your *Goddess Style* lifestyle.

We grew up eating processed foods filled with sugar and chemicals (preservatives and more). That's what we knew. Now, we're making a new choice to rearrange how we approach food in our lives.

Just be mindful of what you're eating and when you see your having an oops moment or even an oops day, stop what you're doing and think. Ask the God and Goddess to give you strength and keep going with your Goddess Style Eating.

Section Two:
Goddess Style Interactions with Food #6

Self-soothing in Ways Other than Food

You've had a hard day at work. You get home. You deserve something soothing. Come on, you've worked hard! Something comforting at this moment would be great.

What do you reach for?

If you said "food," I can relate to that.

After my 20s, I soothed myself with food. I also became sedentary in my daily life. I started packing on the excess pounds.

It's a real conundrum. How do we sooth ourselves without using food?

What can you rely on to help you feel better?

Research shows that creating a replacement-behavior helps when we want to accomplish positive change in our lives. So *merely denying* your desire for ice cream (for example) does *not* work.

What could you put in place of eating?

Recently, my husband bought me a new camera. So, I started up photography again. When I get stir crazy and want to eat everything in sight, I step outside and take photos. I love going out and finding a good subject for a photo. Getting out of the house and away from the kitchen is a great way to stop eating those extra calories. Walking is a bonus; it's a great form of exercise.

So, instead of struggling to keep things *out* of my mouth, I walk, get exercise and have fun doing what I love to do.

Think of things you like to do away from home. In this way, you are replacing food as your comfort. You bring some happiness into your life. Consider taking an improvisation class or, perhaps, a yoga class.

My husband's business coach recently advised him: "When you put something you enjoy in your day, you'll probably need less comfort like seeing three episodes of your favorite show on Netflix."

I've learned that Goddess Style Weight Loss really is about shifting our behavior patterns. Find something to do instead of eating. It can be as simple as going for a walk.

Section Two:
Goddess Style Interactions with Food #7

Are There Spiritual Beings Helping You Right Now?—Reincarnation

"What do you want to learn?"
"Compassion."
"Okay. I can help you with that during your next incarnation...."

My question for you is: *Does the idea of reincarnation connect with your heart on some level?*

We all start in the spirit world as spiritual beings. Before we come down to incarnate into a new body, we talk with our Spirit Guides and other beings. We decide what lessons we want/need to learn. We map them out and place lessons into our upcoming incarnation. Our obstacles have a gift for us.

Working Together with Other Souls

We also work together with other souls to help them learn and grow. We agree before we incarnate who our parents and friends are. Let's say you want to learn compassion. You and another spirit talk and agree that this spirit will help you learn. In your life, you marry this person (spirit), and your spouse creates opportunities for you to learn that lesson. Some can be intense. What if you have a spouse with clinical depression or an addiction to oxycodone? This is an opportunity to learn compassion and forgiveness for your spouse.

What is a Soul Group?

We are grouped with souls that vibrate at the same level as we do (our Soul Group).

One of the great reasons we want to incarnate on the physical plane is to learn lessons and to meet and be influenced by higher vibrating souls. In this way, we hope to raise our own vibrational levels.

Several authors suggest that reincarnating is the opportunity for us to raise the frequency of our vibrational level. It's suggested that at higher levels of vibration we can better connect to deeper levels of the truth. We can then move on to higher realms in the spirit world.

Ideas about the importance of reincarnation arise in Wicca, Buddhism, Hinduism and more.

A view of reincarnation can even bring us comfort. When we hear of children dying, we can hold the view that they will have another opportunity in a future incarnation.

Death is the graduation of the soul to a new life.

May your understanding of reincarnation comfort you.

Section Three
Release Yourself from the Need for Extra Weight to Feel Safe

Imagine making the profound shift from having a big body to protect yourself, and, instead, using your spiritual practice to feel empowered.

It's understandable that many of us, perhaps, subconsciously, chose to eat a lot to get bigger because we had been wounded severely as small children.

Some research suggests that 93% of the decisions we make during a day are done on the subconscious level.

Wiccans have a special advantage: We can do a spell or ritual that directly impacts our soul and subconscious mind.

Section Three:
Release Yourself from the Need for Extra Weight to Feel Safe #1

Wiccans Dropping Excess Weight and Taking the Spiritual Path of Greater Health

Like many souls in the new year, I heard my doctor say, "You must lose weight. The health problems are too severe."

So, in my first week, I ate nothing but veggies and protein. (Okay. I had a little, itty-bitty piece of dark chocolate ... each day. Oh, then there was the peanut butter ...) I was hoping to shed the pounds and be healthier. I exercised every day and ate what the doctor told me to.

However, when I went to the scale to my terror I had gained weight!

Ugh! What a horrible feeling!

So, what can I do?!

Here's a Weight Loss Spell.

What you will need:

- One seven knob, green candle
- Banishing oil
- Candleholder
- Lighter

Warning: Be sure to do this spell during the waning moon.

Cast the Circle.

Cleanse and consecrate the oil and candle. Set the candle in its holder. Sit and meditate on your losing weight. See the candle as a representation of the excess weight. When you're ready, light the candle and say three times:

Little knobbed candle of green,
With powers, great and unseen.
I light you in the vast darkness so,
Illuminate health for me to know.
Bad eating habits and lethargy, I rip out
Of my life within and without!
Let this my prayer be answered now!

I pray that you will, I pray that you must,
For me to lose weight high water or bust!
As you, my little green candle, melts,
So too does my weight and waistline melt.
So mote it be!

Now sit and meditate on losing weight until the first knob is burned completely. Then put out the candle with a snuffer.

Do the Cakes and Wine Ceremony.

Close the Circle.

The Next Steps

On the subsequent day, simply burn the candle and meditate before it. You'll complete your session when the second knob has melted away.

Continue this process for the next five days.

* * * * * *

For those of us who are letting go of extra weight, may this Spell be helpful to you.

Section Three:
Release Yourself from the Need for Extra Weight to Feel Safe #2

Women Take Leadership of Themselves Inside

Imagine that you can let go of the chains of being so concerned about what other people think of you. I realize that this sounds like a tall order. Stay with me.

You shift your thoughts to "How can I improve myself in ways that *I* want to? What are *my* goals? Who do *I* want to be?"

I've really struggled with what the media pushes on us. I look at movie stars and models, and that is not me.

Over the recent two years, I noticed how things were in an uproar when Gal Gadot was cast as Wonder Woman in feature films.

Many comic book fans made a ruckus that she did not look like the voluptuous comic book Wonder Woman image.

Yesterday, I saw the feature film *Wonder Woman* and I feel that she was well-cast! I had the thought that "having to have big breasts is what men want. It's what they desire. It's not what we are as women."

Then, I thought about what the Goddess looks like. If you go back in time, you notice that Goddess was not the frail, skinny image that we see as many female models. They are not even healthy!

So, I ask you: What would be *taking leadership of yourself?*

First, you need to realize on a deep level that You're Worth It. The God and Goddess want you to feel that way.

You are *not* muck on the bottom of society's shoe. You have value.

Second, realize that you must take control. You need to shift your thoughts. When self-doubt arises, you tell yourself, "How would Goddess see me? In this moment, what is good about me? In this moment, what action do I take to continue on MY positive path?"

Third, catch yourself when you say that somebody made you get stuck. Yes, many of us have been battered physically and emotionally. Even if someone yelled at you ten minutes ago, it is in the past. Ask yourself, "What would Goddess do?"

I've asked myself about this. First, I realized She would not stand for abuse. She would live and act FREE. What does this mean? Perhaps, you decide: "Fine. I'm not calling my mother for three days. *I decide* to take a break."

When you take action, you are expressing the Goddess-within. You are creating.

We know that the Three Times Law points out that whatever we put out into the universe comes back upon us.

So, be kind to yourself, my friend. Let the universe send three times that blessing back at you.

Do you have friends that berate you? Go to places where there are positive people. Seek to get a couple of new friends who will treat you with care and respect. How does that happen? You send out care and respect.

A final note: Living on the path of Goddess Style Weight Loss needs to be for YOU. Not your family. Not your significant other.

Trying to diet because you want to "look nice for my boyfriend" (for example) is *not* enough motivation.

Why?

Because you're relying on someone else's opinion. You're actually looking for energy from outside yourself—so that you do what you need to do.

The energy must arise from inside you. Because YOU want to feel strong and to move. YOU want to enjoy being healthy. YOU want to dance with the Goddess!

Where Is Your Safety?

"Where is your safety?" Maria, a friend, asked me.

"I'm working on this." I paused, then continued, "My safety is actually in my relationship with the God and Goddess."

I rely on the God and Goddess to keep me in Their protective arms, as I listen to Their guiding words, and walk on the Sacred Path.

On the other hand, if we look only to our body as the source of our strength, we can get caught up in fear. The body can be hurt. A cold, flu, a fall—you name it.

We need to remember that we are immortal beings in a body that has a shelf life.

So, our real strength resides in our soul. This is where our faith must be strong. The Gods love us and want us to be happy. They also want us to be healthy. They want us to free of heart disease and diabetes.

It's true that we influence the situation as we make healthy decisions.

In a number of areas of this book, I refer to the pattern of people eating a lot and making their body bigger. For a child, that seems to be a logical strategy.

When we can shift from relying on a big body, then we can actually slim down. That's where knowing that the Gods love us comes in.

This comes back to you making the choice to be healthier for YOU. Not anyone else.

The Gods support your choice. They're always on your side—*helping your every baby step along the way.*

They rejoice as you make progress. With every mistake comes a lesson. And learning that lesson makes you stronger. Being stronger helps you be safe.

Here's an example about taking a baby step. In the beginning of my Goddess Style process, I encouraged my family to help me by keeping cookies out of the house. This was creating a "safety zone."

Why did I start in this way? Because I am addicted to sugar and carbs.

Let's pause for a moment and look at the word *addiction.* Dr. Michael F. Roizen wrote about *addiction:*

"… If the behavior has a beneficial effect in the short term but adverse consequences the long term.

"If the person develops a tolerance to the amount of the behavior and then needs more and more of that particular substance or action to achieve those beneficial effects."

So, when I started my journey with Goddess Style, I needed to keep many processed foods *out* of my home. Little by little, I was able to become strong enough to see my family members eating things that I've chosen to exclude from my eating habits.

In summary, think of creating your own "safety zone." Additionally, look to casting a Circle, doing a ritual and connecting with the Gods as your *true source* of strength and safety.

Section Three:
Release Yourself from the Need for Extra Weight to Feel Safe #4

Who Guards You? — A Wiccan Advantage

Feeling alone plagues many of us. This relates to an essential question: Who guards you? You guard you, with the God and Goddess.

Spirit Guides can also assist you. (For more about finding your Spirit Guide, see the "Special Note" section below.) My Spirit Guide is Linda.

The idea of who guards you is a big topic because a significant number of us have, at least subconsciously, overindulged in food to develop a big body as a shield.

Rita, a friend, said, "It was like I was saying, 'See! I'm no longer a tiny girl that you can abuse!"

Think about it. With a big body, the scared, vulnerable you on the inside might feel safe.

As I write about Goddess Style Weight Loss, I observe the idea that dropping weight can be like dropping our shield. Why would we do that when the world proved to us that there are those who have hurt us—and others who might hurt us still?

In place of the big body, what or who will protect us?

The God, Goddess and Spirit Guides are with you always—24/7.

"But I don't feel Their presence!" Rita said.

This is understandable. Why? Because we're often under the assault of "The Monkey Mind." That's the part of our thinking that "chatters" with distractions and fears.

That's the point. We don't feel the presence of God, Goddess and Spirit Guides because we're distracted by The Monkey Mind. (For example, I just felt the urge to check email on my smartphone.)

The answer is to step away from the chattering. For example, my husband meditates for three minutes every morning. Just today, he said, "I didn't feel peace until about 2 minutes and 50 seconds into my meditation. But I did reach the peaceful experience."

The next step is to identify when, where and how you can feel the presence of God, Goddess and Spirit Guides. We see Their presence every day. From the grass between our toes to the Rocky Mountains that are Their cathedrals.

We can Cast a Circle and do a ritual which takes us out of our daily, Monkey Mind, routine.

But what about inside of us?

We are even distracted by feelings in our bodies.

There is a solution: Eat in healthy ways.

Eating healthy helps us run our bodies with the fuel they were meant to have. Goddess, through human history, has provided the bounty that sustains us. It's only in modern times when people have poisoned ourselves with processed, so-called food.

Realize that with healthy eating choices, our bodies will

run better and with that comes a tighter bond in the ever-loving arms of the Gods.

In this way, we will be closer to Them, and we have a better chance of physically feeling Them within ourselves. It's easier to connect with God and Goddess during a meditation if your body is *not* suffering from feeling bloated.

To bring this full circle, we have been talking about who guards you.

You guard yourself by making healthy choices.

Even better, when you do things to reduce the distractions of the Monkey Mind, you open the door to the presence of God, Goddess and Spirit Guides.

Just like being in Circle, you can have a spiritual experience when you go Goddess Style: Eating from the earth and honoring the beings you consume.

The truth is: Having a big body can hold you back from experiences you really want. (I must say at 36.8 pounds lighter, it is easier for me to fit into a seat on a jet plane!)

Having a big body apparently was something I needed at one time.

Now, I'm focused on who really guards me—myself, God and Goddess.

Would you like to make the transition to feeling the presence of God, Goddess and Spirit Guides?

* Special Note ...
How to Meet Your Spirit Guides

"How can I meet my Spirit Guides?" Jessie asked.

"Through meditation," I replied. "While meditating, I had this experience:

I went to the standing stones and asked to meet my Spirit

Guide. Suddenly, I was aware of a loving presence. A beautiful woman came forward. She approached me, and I could see her pleasant features form. Lovely brown hair and eyes came into focus. She reached out and took my hand."

You can receive guidance from your Spirit Guide or even a Totem Animal.

Shaman Elder Maggie Wahls wrote: "A totem animal is often a protector, a mate to travel the Inner Worlds with who knows its way around and can get you in, to your destination and out again safely."

I always start in a safe place on the astral plane. This could be a cottage or a circle of standing stones. Pick a place that has power to protect you. You can meet your Spirit Guide there.

The Witches' Cottage is where I start in my daily meditation. From the Witches' Cottage, you can begin your journey on the astral plane.

Here is a meditation to discover your own Witches' Cottage.

(The below material is an excerpt from my book, *Goddess Has Your Back*.)

Witches' Cottage Meditation

1) Cast the Circle.

Note: This meditation includes special pauses. During a pause, you have the time to interact with the environment of the Witch's Cottage on the astral plane. Consider either having a friend read the directions to you or pre-recording the material in your own voice for later playback. When you come across the words "Short pause" do not say them aloud. Simply pause your reading before you move onward.

2) Witches' Cottage Meditation

Relax. Take a deep breath in. Breathe out, releasing the stresses of the day. Keep taking deep breaths, in and out. With each exhale, you get more and more relaxed. Feel your body as it sits comfortably Notice now that the light slowly begins to dim. You feel comfortable and at peace as the light continues to fade. Now the light is gone and you are happy and secure in the darkness.

(Short pause)

Soon you notice the light starts to return. Slowly at first. Then as your eyes adjust to the new light, you now can see that you are in a Cottage. The air is fresh and clean. Look around to orient yourself to your new surroundings. Look to the south wall and see a warm, friendly fire crackling in a large stone fireplace. Walk to the fireplace and enjoy the light and warmth the fire gives you. Observe the fireplace What kind of stone is it made of? What kind of kindling is being used?

(1-minute pause)

Look to your right and notice the west wall and then walk to it and see a nearby fountain. What does this fountain look like? How was it constructed?

(1-minute pause)

Look to your right and see the north wall and walk to it.
Near the wall is a large stone table. Observe the table. What distinguishing marks does it have?

(1-minute pause)

Turn to your right again and view the east wall. Walk to it and now see a well-kept window set into the wall. What can you see out of the window? What time of day or night is it?

(1-minute pause)

Further explore the cottage. What does it smell like? What materials were used in its construction? How many rooms do you see?

(5 minutes pause)

Know that this is a safe and secure place where no one and nothing may enter without your permission. You find a nice place to sit. Rest a while. Then notice how the light starts dimming. Feel comfortable and at peace as the light continues to fade. Now, the light is gone, and you are happy and secure in the darkness.

(Short Pause)

Soon, you notice that the light starts to return. Slowly at first. Your eyes adjust to the new light and you feel safe, calm and refreshed. Now open your eyes to your present-day world.

3) Do the Cakes and Wine Ceremony
4) Close the Circle

The Witches' Cottage serves as a safe place when you

start traveling on the astral plane.

My process is to begin at my Witches' Cottage and then go to the standing stones.

You can use another process, but still *make sure* that you begin with a safe place.

Section Four
Be Smart about Having Energy

What are sources of energy which are especially available to Wiccans? Special prayers, rituals and chants.

Section Four:
Be Smart about Having Energy #1

New Years' Resolutions Booster Prayer

Some say March is where New Years' Resolutions go to die.

No more!

Here is my special prayer for you:

New Years' Resolutions Booster Prayer

As fire glows,
Inspiration grows.

As ocean tides flow,
Blocks to my desire go.
As the wind blows
My new life knows.
As the soil's fertile
I go over my hurdle.
So mote it be.

Blessings to you.

Section Four:
Be Smart about Having Energy #2

How Can You Support Someone Who Is Grieving?

Why is grieving and being smart about your own energy related? Imagine how much anguish many of us feel as we worry about doing the "right thing" when our friend or family member is grieving.

When we worry about doing the right thing, we're, in effect, "leaking energy."

Think about it. Much of the time when we say we're stressed out, it's connected to our interactions with significant people in our lives.

We've be taught that "if your friend feels bad, of course, you should feel bad, too."

Some Wiccans are empaths. We feel other people's pain. We note that having compassion is important. Still, we need to be careful that we do *not* allow ourselves to be truly drained of our precious energy.

At my blog GoddessHasYourBack.com, I first introduced some ideas about guarding your personal energy ....

"What can I do to support Jimmy? I just ... I just don't know how to help a friend who's suffering so much when losing a family member. What can I say?" my friend, Fred, asked.

"It's not about saying the perfect words. It's about being present. It's more about listening," I replied.

Have you noticed that when someone dies, some people just disappear? That is, some friends and family leave because they cannot sit and experience the pain while being there for the grieving person.

We, as Wiccans, can call upon the God and Goddess to strengthen us so we can endure. You don't even need to say anything. Just be there.

You can say prayers asking for your own strength to be augmented.

Or you can ask the fellow Wiccan if he or she wants you to express this following prayer:

Prayer to Heal After a Loss

Lord and Lady give us strength; let us heal from the loss of _____.

Bring us comfort during this harrowing time.

Let us learn what we can from the loss of _____ *and find peace within us.*

May we endure as the grief goes through its seasons.

Let us be transformed with love at this time.

In the Lord and Lady, we ask.

So mote it be.

May this be of service to you.

Section Four:
Be Smart about Having Energy #3

A Goddess Viewpoint on Eating and Television

A number of researchers note that eating while distracted can lead to us consuming 10% more calories*. Distractions like television, reading, or being active on one's computer take up our conscious attention. We just don't notice how much we're shoving in our piehole.

What is the solution? We consciously choose to become *mindful* of how we eat.

Being mindful is also important related to late night eating. More research suggests that late night eating results in many of us consuming 25% more calories.

Oh, my Goddess!

* research about eating 10% more was noted in the *American Journal of Clinical Nutrition.*

Recently, I asked a couple of friends, who eat while watching TV, "Why do you do that?"

"I'm not sure. I guess I'm just looking for comfort after a tough day at work," Sarah said.

"Eating and watching TV is fun," Mark said. He likes to eat popcorn while watching a movie on Netflix. But then he pauses the film and goes for cookies. Oh, well ...

Let's begin with the comment about "comfort."

I've noticed that when I do a Candle Lighting Ritual, I feel peace and gratefulness.

My point is that we can go directly to the source of comfort by asking Goddess for peace during a Candle Lighting Ritual or during meditation.

Goddess Style Weight Loss invites us to choose replacements for standard, processed food (loaded with carbs and chemicals) that we might eat.

Let's say a person is about to eat four "sticks" of Prosciutto Wrapped Grilled String Cheese. She can stop and do a candle lighting ritual.

Or she could just stop and say a prayer of gratitude to the Goddess. By taking this time to focus, she can pay attention to what is in front of her.

The point is to become mindful.

When we're mindful, we can decide to put two of the Prosciutto sticks back into the package and return the package to the refrigerator.

Finally, just before you consume anything, say a prayer and give thanks to God and Goddess for the bounty you have. This helps you stay focused on what you're about to eat.

You avoid mindless eating (like eating popcorn in front of the TV).

This is a helpful shift to keep you in the process of

Goddess Style Weight Loss.

Eating less is more. By this I mean, when you eat less, you gain more confidence.

You gain another step toward your goal-weight.

You gain improved health.

Section Five
Create Lots of Self-Care and Comfort (so food fades into the background)

"I don't know how I'll ever stop stuffing my face," Rita, a friend, said. "Do you have any ideas for me?"

"It's important to find comforting parts of life that do *not* involve food," I began.

"Is that even possible?" she said, with a rueful smile.

"We, Wiccans, have ritual, meditation, walking near trees, creating a sigil and more. I realize that we might not get that 'rush of comfort' from some of these activities ... at first."

Section Five:
Create Lots of Self-Care and Comfort (so food fades into the background) #1

Reach Out to God and Goddess in Stressful Times

A number of my Wiccan friends (and other friends with

other spiritual paths) are stressing out now. Can you blame them?

Just today, one of my friends sent information about nine bills up for a vote in the U.S. House of Representatives. The bills are designed to take away vital services from low income people.

I have Wiccan friends who are terrified about what will happen to them when they lose the healthcare provided the Affordable Care Act (which is stated to have provided roughly 20 million people with health insurance who did *not* have it before).

I am deeply concerned, and I participated in a rally (staged in front of Congresswoman Anna Eschoo's office) to emphasize our request for continued healthcare coverage. I was even called up to speak briefly at the microphone.

That afternoon, for a brief time, I felt my worry quiet down. Why? I was participating. My concern is that, although we can participate in activism, we still live much of the time with intense pressure.

With the negative changes, many of us feel like our inner self is being squashed. What can we do? Sometimes, a good cry may help. Still, the God and Goddess are there for us. It's time for us to reach out to Them.

Asking the Gods for Inner Peace

1. You can meditate

A number of us can use meditation to go into a deep trance and meet the God and Goddess. Ask for Their guidance. You'll often find comfort.

Several Wiccans have asked God and Goddess to quell the fire of fear that resides inside.

Consider the practices of grounding and centering to

relieve much anxiety you may have. You can release stress by simply deep breathing and placing your feet flat on the floor. Release the energy by visualizing that you are pushing the energy into the earth. Mother Earth will recycle it for you.

Grounding can help us get to a point where we're calm about those things we cannot control. We're not feeling good. Still, we're okay. I've seen authors write about the difference between acceptance and approval. I certainly do NOT approve of those actions that hurt people. For a moment of peace, I can accept that, in this moment, I am okay.

You can do this Inner Peace Ritual

What you will need:

- White candle
- Candle holder
- Gardenia Incense (for peace)
- Gardenia oil (you can use extra virgin olive oil if you can't get gardenia oil)
- Regular ritual tools
- Cakes and wine

Cast Circle in the usual manner. Cleanse and consecrate the white candle. Then as you dress the candle with the gardenia oil, visualize how you want peace. See in your mind people respectfully talking to each other and agreeing. Place the candle in the its holder—in middle of your altar.

Light the candle and say three times:

Goddess
Help us see
Our graceful connection.
Bless us with your clarity
Turn hard hearts to charity.

Sit and continue your visualization as you watch the candle burn. Let the candle burn down until it has been fully consumed.

Do the Cakes and Wine Ceremony.

Close the Circle.

You can repeat this ritual to support you and the world around you.

Section Five:
Create Lots of Self-Care and Comfort (so food fades into the background) #2

Wiccans Stand in the Face of Fear and Uncertainty

"I don't know what to do! I'm scared about what's going to happen soon," Jake said.

"Is it—?" I began.

"It's this new administration. The new President and his buddies are going to take everything apart, and I'm going to get hurt. I'm worried about my health insurance and–" Jake said.

With this upcoming administration coming into the White House (President Elect of 2017) a lot of people are downright scared of what will happen. I know I am. As a witch, I fear for the environment and for my friends in my community. I also have other friends in other communities who are afraid that their rights will be snatched away.

I have fears about the safety of our water and other

things.

With so much fear, how can someone combat the storm of uncertainty that is all around us?

I have created this simple ritual to help many us connect with God and Goddess. This can lead to some calmness and restful nights of sleep.

What you will need:

- One white candle
- White sage incense
- One white flower
- Amethyst crystal
- Altar pentacle
- Candle holder
- Wine or juice
- Cakes

Cast Circle in the usual manner.

Cleanse and consecrate the flower, crystal, and candle.

Place the flower and the crystal on the pentacle and say:

May peace be around me.

Insert the candle into candle holder and place them on top of the pentacle. Light the candle. Then kneel and say:

Goddess holds me,
God enfolds me.
I want to be clear,
With fear, ever near.
Give me the power to fight,
Remove darkness, be all right.
Have my heart set sail.

Let love prevail.
So mote it be.

Do the Cakes and Wine Ceremony.

Close the Circle.

* * *

May this ritual bring you comfort, clarity and the energy to move forward.

Section Five:
Create Lots of Self-Care and Comfort (so food fades into the background) #3

Release Worry Chant

Here's a chant to help you in becoming free of worry.

The Release Worry Chant

Worry, worry in my mind
Cluttering my thoughts all the time.
What goes in, must come out,
Creating better feelings all about.
Goddess, release me,
Show me the way.
Goddess, release me,
Brighten my day.

Moonwater SilverClaw

Section Five:
Create Lots of Self-Care and Comfort (so food fades into the background) #4

Wiccans Invoke Peace

As I listened to the news—

WASHINGTON — The United States has attacked a Syrian air base with roughly 60 cruise missiles in response to a chemical weapons attack it blames on President Bashar Assad. Officials are reporting that the Russians knew of the airstrikes in advance.
—ABC7News

—my heart ached. People destroyed by chemical weapons and cruise missiles. People running the USA decided to attack individuals of another country.

What can we, as Wiccans, do to help bring back some peace into the world right now?

Simple Peace Ritual

When to do this ritual:
Full moon (I would suggest this coming full moon.)

What you will need:
- 1 white candle
- 1 white rose
- Peace oil (You can use extra virgin olive oil if you don't have it.)
- White feathers to decorate altar (optional)
- 1 red apple
- Rose incense
- Pin

Place the white rose, candle and red apple in the center of your altar.

Cast Circle in the usual manner.

Cleanse and consecrate your white candle, rose and red apple with the incense and holy water. (Witches make their own holy water with three pinches of salt.)

Dress your white candle with your oil, and place it in its holder in the middle of your altar.

Take up your pin and punch in the letters of the word *peace* into the apple, while saying:

As I open my heart to peace, so to may those in conflict open their hearts to peace with each other.

Take up the white rose and kiss it, saying:

May this peace be as pure as the white rose I hold now.

Concentrate now on the white candle. Think of the tempers of those who are in charge and who are creating the current crisis of violence. Imagine their consciousness filling with the White Light of Peace. Lighting the candle, say:

Candle of White, listen to my words. The White Rose has spoken to those whose hearts are now opened. Let peace replace the hate within. May the God and Goddess's love prevail.
So mote it be!

Pick up the apple. Take a bite and envision the White Light of the Gods' Love surrounds you.

As you sit and eat the apple, envision that peace rests in your heart.

Do the Cakes and Wine Ceremony.

Close the Circle.

May this ritual bring peace to all those who need it.

Section Six
Protect Yourself

What does it take to stay in your process of Goddess Style Weight Loss? Energy! Wiccans have an advantage in that we can take effective action to protect ourselves. As we protect ourselves, we protect our energy. Personal strength is part of energy. Let's face it: Strength is necessary for our Goddess Style Weight Loss journey.

Section Six:
Protect Yourself #1

How You Can Stop Hexes and Curses— The Witch's Bottle

Years ago, fearing that she was being attacked by someone wielding a curse, one of my readers contacted me. What was the solution in that particular situation? A Witch's Bottle.

A Witch's Bottle can help protect you from hexes, curses and other baneful spells.

How do you make a Witch's Bottle?

What you will need:

- Wide-mouthed bottle
- Iron nail
- Copper tacks
- Pins and other sharp objects
- The victim's (the person under attack) urine or you can use apple cider vinegar.
- Sealing wax

What to do:

Clean the bottle and fill it with the iron nail, copper tacks and other objects. Add urine (or apple cider vinegar*) to cover the objects in the jar.

Use the sealing wax to permanently shut the bottle's top. Identify a place on your property where you can confidently bury the bottle because you know it will not be disturbed.

Say this phrase:

May this Witch's Bottle protect me and keep me safe from those who would do me harm. May my health and happiness be overflowing. So Mote It Be.

Bury the bottle.

If you don't have a yard or somewhere to do this, you can bury the bottle in a potted plant. Now, you have something portable; you can take it with you if you move.

*if you use apple cider vinegar use a taglock

(traditionally, it was some hair, but it could be something of the person like fingernail clippings, blood, etc.)

May you stay safe and happy.

Section Six:
Protect Yourself #2

The Wiccan's Way of Protection from Car Accidents

As I stood absolutely still, I held my breath. The technician did an X-ray of my whiplashed neck. I thought, "Why?! Why did I let it come to this?"

I had been rear-ended by a car just a short while before. A sedan car had cut me off. I brought my car to a gradual stop. The car driver behind me should have had ample time to come to a safe stop. But, No! Slam—she rear-ended my car.

Just great.

Here's something worse. Some months ago, I thought, "I need to do a car blessing."

Did I do it?

No.

That's how I ended up placed against this X-ray machine.

So, I've written this Car Blessing for you and me to do better in life.

Car Blessing
What you will need:

- Water
- Salt
- Lighter or matches
- Bowl
- Red candle
- Sage bundle

Bless the water and salt. Put three pinches of salt into the water. Stir three times clockwise, and this holy water is now ready. Bless the sage bundle by lightly dabbing you fingers in the holy water and then asperge the bundle. Bless the flame of the red candle.

Dip your fingers into the bowl of holy water, asperge the car, and say:

I bless this car with Water and Earth that it remains safe from all harm.

Use the red candle flame to light the sage bundle. Waft the smoke over the car and say:

I bless this car with Air and Fire that it remains safe from all harm. Lord and Lady, may this car and its occupants be safe and free from any harm from outside and inside forces.

So Mote It Be.

May this blessing keep you safe.

Section Six:
Protect Yourself #3

The Wiccan's Salve in a Car Accident

A bright cheery day—I didn't know what shadow would come my way.

I brought the family car to a stop at a red light. I glanced at my Dad. He was in good spirits. We just completed getting the car washed. We were homeward bound.

My car was in one of two left-turn lanes. To my right was a sedan car also preparing to turn left. The light signaled "green" for me to execute the left turn.

The sedan cut off our car, making an illegal U-turn.

I brought the car to a gradual stop, giving ample time for the car behind me to respond to the situation.

CRUNCH—the car behind me rear-ended our car.

My neck snapped back.

All that I could do was think of the Gods. I prayed to the Gods that the outcome of this accident would *not* be as extreme as I thought it was.

I said something like: "Lord and Lady, may this be *not* as bad as it seems."

I'm grateful to note that my father was *not* injured. Considering that my neck injury was significant, that was great news. Apparently, the headrest was set at just the right level to help him. Mine, on the other hand, doesn't touch the back of my head so I got a serious case of whiplash.

I'm healing. But our car still needs work.

When unexpected trouble arrives, remember the God and Goddess are here to support you in times of need.

Section Six:
Protect Yourself #4

The Wiccan First Aid Kit—a Lesson in the Mountains

The air crisp, snow on the mountains, I glance at my Dad. Eighty years old, he's spry enough on this coarse and slippery trail.

It's his birthday month, and we are camping at Pinecrest. Dad grew up here. He loved playing in the woods around this lake, that we're now circling on foot.

Small streams cross the trail ahead. Because of the record rain fall in California, the snow pack has grown thick in the Sierras. More water melts from the snow pack than usual.

The soil softened by the runoff gives way beneath my father's right foot. He topples. His face slams into a rock. Blood pours out of the gash on his forehead.

I've got nothing. Nothing to staunch the bleeding. What would you do?

As Wiccans, we love the natural world. Like me, many go

camping and hiking. We bring many things with us: Shelter, food, water and more.

But I made a mistake. I failed to carry some kind of first aid kit on that hike. Make sure that you always carry a first aid kit in the woods.

We did make it to the ER, and my Dad is okay. Bruised and healing.

But what about daily life, with its disappointments and fear? This is where a Wiccan First Aid Kit would be handy.

The Wiccan's First Aid Kit

The Wiccan's first aid kit can include:

Meditation
Meditation provides a great healing salve for many worries.

Protection Charm
A protection charm can help you ward off certain mishaps.

Aromatherapy
Consider having an aromatherapy necklace to enhance your inner peace.

You can add other items to your own Wiccan's First Aid Kit.

Section Six:
Protect Yourself #5

When the World Around You is Crazy

What to do? Doesn't it feel like the whole world has gone off the deep end? With people getting bombed to the political unrest in America, we now find ourselves in complete world chaos.

I am sooo stressed that I have been eating things I shouldn't. Even my immediate surroundings are inundated with drama. For example, some of my friends have broken up their lifelong friendships.

Certain moments of the day, I feel torn apart. I need to be in three places at once: Helping my sweetheart … and … helping a friend with moving … and … helping another friend with a BIG project. Even my parents are having a difficult time.

I admit it. My oops days are too close together. I was on a great trend of dropping weight, but in the last two days I've fallen back and gained 3 pounds!

So, when it feels like the world has fallen apart, what do we do?

It's time to turn to the God and Goddess for strength. It's important to do some real self-care. Why? When you're a mess, you don't have the energy to be helpful to anyone else. It's time to slow down, meditate and find your inner calmness.

How do we do that? You can light some incense and play some pleasant calming music as a first step. Next, practice the process of grounding. Bring your awareness back into the quiet center in yourself. Concentrate on your breath and begin to meditate. Call upon the God and Goddess for the strength to not only endure, but, to thrive with peace in your heart and mind at this stressful time.

Once you have done this, you may want to take a ritual bath. In this way you will shed the unhealthy energy from your body and spirit.

Afterwards, eating something nutritious will also help you ground. Take your time and enjoy the process.

Caring for yourself is a vital key to helping others. Find the peace that resides within you, and share such positive energy with other people.

Section Six:
Protect Yourself #6

Wiccans Use Self-Care to Enhance Their Lives

What do you want? You can discover how Wicca is a powerful tool for transforming your life. It turns out that Wicca and self-care are closely related. Now, we'll look at modes in which Wicca can help you manifest the best in life:

1. Body

Wicca teaches us that our body is a temple. Many Wiccans decorate their body-temple with makeup, dyed hair, and tattoos. Still, a vital way to care for our temple is with conscious choices about what we put inside our body.

Think about what you eat, drink and breathe. Many Wiccans avoid taking various drugs because of potential damage to their sacred body.

Related to what we eat, I'm currently being careful about my nutrition. I only eat what comes from the womb and from the ground. That is, I avoid processed foods. In this way, I've dropped 36.8 lbs. of excess body weight. Yes, I'm rather delighted about that!

Eating natural fruits, veggies and proteins keeps your body in good working order.

Making good choices and taking care with what you eat demonstrate love for your body.

Let's not forget exercise. Make it simple. I walk at least one hour each day. Exercise and good nutrition keep your body tuned and help you build energy for spells.

Taking a simple walk in nature (even at a local park) can enhance your health. Being in nature is being in "church" for us, Wiccans. When we surround ourselves with flora and fauna, we experience the heightened presence of the God and Goddess.

2. Mind

Wiccans care for their mind through meditation. Meditation assists us to practice focus, which is necessary for successful spells. My meditation practice has nurtured my growth in ways that I could not imagine. Meditation even helped me leave an abusive marriage.

Consider adding meditation (even just five minutes a day) to enhance your life.

3. Spirit

Through taking action to conduct rituals and other Wiccan practices, we evolve spiritually. Doing magick for our own personal change creates transformation within our spirit.

What does taking care of our spirit mean? It means doing actions like meditating, holding Circle, and conducting rituals. Then what happens? You become closer to the God and Goddess. You learn the lessons you came here to learn. The God and Goddess can more easily guide you. How? You have lifted yourself up to a higher level through your conscientious efforts with Wiccan practices. God and Goddess can guide us to the answers we seek.

Remember, Wiccan practices are tied with good self-care. As you get stronger and healthier, you also empower yourself as a witch.

Section Six:
Protect Yourself #7

Wiccans Dealing with Prejudice

"How do I become less prejudiced?" one of my readers asked.

That's a powerful question.

As I was thinking about replying to the reader, I had some conversations with my sweetheart; he is a person of color. He noted, "Many of us feel that we're free of prejudice. But if you observe closely: A person who intellectually tries to be free of prejudice can still exhibit a physical 'flinch.' A big flinch can be when an older woman pulls her purse closer to herself when a person of a different race sits in an adjoining chair. A smaller flinch can be when a person's face shows a wince when that person sees two people of a different race approach."

I have a number of friends who consider themselves to be free of prejudice. Still, when certain topics come up they become angry, and they have a lot of judgments and grievances against certain individuals.

"It's hard to be tolerant of people who are not tolerant of you."
— Marianne Williamson

We, Wiccans, find that we face intolerance from people who have been told by their religious leaders that witches are less than (or worse) than others. I admit it. In the past when someone has spouted off about witches and said truly ignorant things, I had some judgments about that person.

As Wiccans, we work with the Shadow-Self (the dark side of oneself that one does NOT want to look at). We can bring light to the Shadow-Self, and I'm going to share Three Steps to Free Yourself of Prejudice.

"It is better to light a candle than curse the darkness."
— Eleanor Roosevelt

The following Three Steps help you shine light on the Shadow-Self, understand yourself a bit more, and, perhaps, change in positive ways.

Three Steps to Free Yourself of Prejudice

1. Have good experiences with people who are different from you.

Many times, our prejudices manifest because of having bad experiences or just hearing about bad experiences. Often, people form prejudices when they have had NO experiences with other people who seem so different.

Many Wiccans complain about those people who show contempt for witches without knowing what Wicca really is.

We, Wiccans, can stretch and make a neutral space so we

can learn about those people who seem so different from us.

The question is: How does one have good experiences with people unlike ourselves?

Perhaps, you might get involved with a group centered on one of your interests. You might strike up a casual conversation with another group member who seems different from you. Many of us find that it helps when we get out and learn about other cultures/creeds/orientations for ourselves. We learn to avoid letting stereotypes box in our thoughts and feelings.

2. Begin genuine friendships with people different from you.

I have a Caucasian friend who grew up in the South (in a southern state of the USA).

It bothered her that she grew up surrounded by certain Caucasian individuals who daily spouted disparaging remarks about African Americans.

My friend took action. She joined the NAACP; she was often the only Caucasian person in the room. She later moved to California, and continued developing more friendships with African American people. She says, "People are people."

Getting to know people is a good start. This will give you a deeper appreciation for others with differences.

3. Study another culture's positive aspects and let go of stereotypes.

It is sometimes amazing how fast people are quick to judge on little fragments of information. One of my friends told me about how some workaholics deride cultures that have an afternoon siesta. Then, this friend worked in a particular bank that had a lounge area where employees could take a nap during their noon break. These employees came back to work with more energy. They proved to be more productive.

Here's the point. One can look into the history of the siesta. It's reported that the siesta began as a way to help people in a hot climate avoid two hours of the hottest weather. This was a wise practice to protect the health of local people. Additionally, it was a way to reclaim energy before one went back to work.

So, it's true that if one knows more, one may avoid being quick to judge.

In summary, you can use the above Three Steps to help free yourself of negative prejudicial thoughts.

Still, the real solution can be found in my friend's example. She went out of her way to have friends of a different racial background.

So, I invite you to be a candle in the darkness.

Section Six:
Protect Yourself #8

Keep Learning and Expand Your Power to Protect Yourself

Recently, one of my readers asked, "How can I practice witchcraft and follow the Wiccan religion?"

My first thought is: "It's interesting that this reader separated two elements of Wicca."

I suggest that witchcraft *is* the religion. Still, I feel that without Casting the Circle, conducting rituals, practicing magick, one is *not* fully following the Wiccan religion.

Here's my point: Wicca is honoring the old Gods and Goddesses. Part of honoring them and growing into our full potential is the practice of magick.

In essence, Wicca is *not* just a scholarly activity. Wicca is a faith of doing. Wicca is an experiential path. You experience the Gods and Goddesses. You are *not* simply acquiescing to being told there are Gods and Goddesses.

Now, we have a sub-question here: "How can I begin a

practice of witchcraft?" Many people start on the Path by reading books. (I'm so glad that you're reading this book.)

In this way, you can see if the Path is right for you. A book I recommend starting with is *The Hidden Children of the Goddess*. It is a Wicca 101 book. Consider *Which Witch is Which?* as a book to explore some of the different traditions of Wicca/witchcraft.

If you are looking for traditional witchcraft, you need to find a mentor because many elders will *not* teach it over the Internet.

In my own coven, we conduct in-person learning opportunities. Learn as much as you can. I have a reading list on my blog GoddessHasYourBack.com. You may want to start there. A number of books on that list help you learn to protect yourself from negative energy.

Section Six:
Protect Yourself #9

How to Handle the Holidays (and Buffets)

Just today, I was having Father's Day dinner with my parents and husband. I turned to my mother and said, "I can have a potato skin because today is a special day."

My mom smiled and said: "It has cheese on it," she offered, aiming to be helpful.

Basically, we were trying to justify my choosing to have some carbohydrates. Normally, I avoid eating carbohydrates.

For example, four days ago, during dinner, my husband enjoyed a bit of mashed potatoes.

In response, I slathered my grilled chicken breast with guacamole!

That was a good choice for me.

When I was talking with my doctor, we covered the idea that there are "good fats." Apparently, avocados contain "good fats."

The idea is to choose to have a moderate amount of foods that contain good fats.

One friend said, "I've learned to eat what I want on the actual holiday. And, I eat in a healthy way on the days *before* the actual day and the days *after* the actual day."

Some Methods for Dinning at a Buffet

Some years ago, I'd see my husband place just a table spoon of potato salad, a tiny portion of fish and many other items on his buffet dinner plate.

"What are you doing?" I asked.

"It's an opportunity. I want to enjoy the taste of many things. And still, I need to keep the total amount of food down to a wise amount," he said.

Good idea.

You can choose to have a small portion of a number of items.

This requires me to get over the "eat it all" and "clear your plate" admonishments I grew up with—at my parents' dinner table.

I tell myself: "Look, the restaurant will toss out the excess food tonight, anyway. I'll just take a bit—and protect my health."

Section Seven
Be Smart about Keeping Yourself Strong and Free of Energy-Drainers

What do you need to stay on the path of Goddess Style Weight Loss? You need extra energy. Where do you get that energy? From the Sun God and the Element of Fire ...

Section Seven:
Be Smart about Keeping Yourself Strong and Free of Energy-Drainers #1

The Power of the God of Summer

"I'm feeling edgy," my friend, Janet, said, during a phone call.

An hour later, my husband said, "I'm really energized. I'm on my way to finishing a draft of the book I'm working on."

I reflected on this and noted that these two moments

actually tune into something occurring on the cosmic level. To our ancestors, Beltane celebrates the beginning of Summer. As the Wheel turns to Midsummer, the God is at the peak of His Power.

Traditional Witches emphasize having a balance of male and female energies. Still, we can take advantage of the seasons and the surge of masculine power or feminine power. Since this is the time of the God, this is a time of more masculine power.

Since every human being has both male and female energies in them, women can take advantage of this time, too. For the sake of our conversation, let's look on "masculine energy" as a "let's go!-energy."

Here's a chant to help you embrace this time of the God.

For this chant, we embrace the "doing energy" as embodied in the Element of Fire.

The Sun gains power,
This is my hour.
Actions manifest desire.
As bright as a bonfire,
My Will, the multiplier.
In Your Great Hour,
Lord, lift me higher.
So Mote It Be.

May this chant empower you to take action and improve your daily life.

Section Seven:
Be Smart about Keeping Yourself Strong and Free of Energy-Drainers #2

The Wiccan Path to Support and Comfort During Tough Times

"This doesn't make sense. Fred was such a good man. Why did he die so young?" my friend Danny asked me.

"I grieve with you. Just saying the usual words probably won't help right now," I began.

Later in our conversation, we talked about reincarnation. My view is: We are all here to learn lessons. With the view of reincarnation, all things fit together. For example, a child, who dies at six-years-old, can return and have another lifetime in which she grows up, gets married and has many adventures.

Still, it's hard to endure one's own suffering and even feelings of anguish when loved ones are suffering. Let's take it even further: Why do the Gods allow innocent children to die in tsunamis or other situations?

Here is a possible explanation: In the Summerlands, before we incarnate we gather with other souls. We agree on helping each other to learn our lessons in the next incarnation. You might say that, together, we come up with a plan before our next incarnation.

It breaks my heart to hear of people dying in a disaster. Then I hear one of my friends say, "That disaster just reminded me how life is short and how we need to cherish each other in what little time we have."

In the Summerlands, some souls agree to go through hardship in order to help us learn lessons that we couldn't learn by ourselves. Some lessons only hit home when extreme things happen. Some souls agree to help others learn compassion. Other souls want to help us learn how to come back from tragedy. Additionally, I noticed that there is a certain type of comfort that can only be experienced when a friend is comforting another person who is reeling from tragedy.

You can do simple rituals to deal with suffering.

Dealing with Suffering Ritual

What you will need:

- One gray candle (you can use red if you can't find gray)
- One green candle
- One white candle
- Three candle holders
- Heat-safe surface
- Healing Oil (to dress candles)
- Altar tools
- Cakes and wine for cakes and wine ceremony

Cast Circle in the usual manner.

Cleanse and consecrate your candles and oil.
Place the three candle holders on the heat-safe surface.
Place the gray candle into the left-side candle holder.
Put the green candle into the middle candle holder, and place the white candle into the right-side candle holder.

Light the gray candle while saying:

With tears of sorrow I see thee,
Suffering—the bane of Earth's peoples.

Light the green candle and say:

With the light cast by this candle
I invite you Gods and Goddesses
To spread comfort and healing to those who are suffering.
Let the people know the love that surrounds them.

Light the white candle and say:

The light of this candle sends purifying energy to
All who need comfort and support.
So mote it be.

Do the Cakes and Wine Ceremony.
Close the Circle.

** **Special Note:** Be sure to have the candles burn down completely. Do NOT leave unattended candles. Be safe.

May this ritual be helpful to you.

Section Seven:
Be Smart about Keeping Yourself Strong and Free of Energy-
Drainers #3

Keep Up My Strength Chant

For those of us who seek better health in the process of
dropping excess weight:

Keep Up My Strength Chant

Power by the Silver Moon
Persistence is the great boon.
Losing weight that had cocooned,
My beauty had been consumed.
The Beauty that is me,
Step Forward Now.
Oh, how lovely You are Now.

Section Eight
Attract Something You Want

Why would we discuss attracting something in a book to help you with weight loss?

I've noticed that there have been times in my life that I turned to food because I felt like I wasn't getting enough—enough praise, enough attention, and enough comfort.

Do you relate to that?

What if you could attract what you really wanted?

What if your life was *so full of good stuff* that food just became a small part of your expansive life?

Fortunately, we, Wiccans, can master the magickal path of attracting the good parts of life. Here's a good place to start.

Section Eight:
Attract Something You Want #1

Where Should I Start Practicing Magick?

Working with candles provides a great way to ease into

magick. Such work can be simple yet powerful. Wiccans often use Chime candles for spellwork. These candles are specifically used for candle magick. Although spellcasters can use other candles, I suggest that you start with Chime candles. You can find them in metaphysical shops or online.

So, once you have some Chime candles, you can use the color guide below to select a color that is appropriate for your spell.

Here is an excerpt about colors and candle magick— from my book, *The Hidden Children of the Goddess.*

Colors and Candle Magick

Let's begin with the meanings of the different candle colors.

Note that the following list is not the final word on color. For instance, the color blue may have another meaning to you than the one listed here. Remember that your mind is your greatest tool. Trust your instincts when your feelings about a specific color differ from what others may advise you.

Here is a list of colors and a brief summary of their general attributes.

- Red: sex, desire, vitality, strength
- Orange: charm, confidence, joy, jealousy, persuasion
- Yellow: intellectual development, joy, intellectual strength
- Green: prosperity, abundance, fertility, money matters
- Blue: healing, protection, spiritual development
- Purple: the occult, power, magick

- Pink: love, friendship, compassion
- White: purity, innocence, peace, tranquility
- Black: decrease, death, revenge, retribution, contacting the dead

Note: I strongly recommend that you never use a black candle. The exceptions are at Samhain or when talking to the dead. Remember the Law of Three [Avoid doing things that harm others].

A candle that has been used for a specific purpose should never be used for a different purpose. Also, it is preferable to burn down the candle all the way. Try to do this in one session. Otherwise, it is acceptable to use the same candle again—but only for the same spell.

* * *

Charging Your Candle

After you choose the candle with an appropriate color, you will then cleanse and consecrate your candle.

Here is an excerpt from one of my posts at my blog GoddessHasYourBack.com

Using Holy Water

After Casting Circle, you hold the object and sprinkle holy water* upon it (the process of asperging). Say: *I cleanse you by Earth and Water.*

* *Wiccans make holy water with three pinches of salt.*

Using Smoke Arising from Incense

Waft the object through the smoke arising from Blessed Incense. By the way, wafting the object through smoke is the process of charging the object.

As you waft the object through smoke three times, say: *I bless and consecrate you by Fire and Air.*

You have made the object suitable for use in your spellwork.

* * *

Now, it is the time to dress your candle. You can use olive oil or a specific oil that helps your spell. For example, you can use Money Drawing Oil for a money spell.

How to Dress a Candle

What do I mean by dress a candle? This is when you rub the candle with oil.

You can use many different types of oils, available at your local metaphysical shop or online. If you don't know which oil to use, simply start with virgin olive oil.

How to Rub the Oil on Your Candle

If you're trying to draw something to you, rub from the tip (wick end) to the base of the candle. This motion draws what you want towards you. To push something away from you (like getting rid of a cold), rub the oil from the base to the wick.

* * *

Now, place your candle in an appropriate candle holder on a heat proof surface (usually on an altar). Focus on what you want the candle to do for you. Hold your hands over the candle as you do this. Next, either express a chant for your spell or light the candle. Meditate on your desire as you watch the flame. Stay with your candle until it burns itself out. It is important to let the candle burn out completely. This seals the spell.

May candle magick bless your days.

Section Eight:
Attract Something You Want #2

A Goddess Viewpoint about Your Desire to Reward Yourself

The Charge of the Goddess by Doreen Valiente includes:

"Let my worship be within the heart that rejoices, for behold, all acts of love and pleasure are My rituals."

From this, we realize that the Goddess wants us to be happy.

When you do something good, wouldn't you say that you'd like to be rewarded? You probably remember a time when you received some kind of reward or celebration for something you accomplished.

Have you thought about it that you provide the hands and feet for the Goddess in this world? Who will reward you? Pragmatically, you can reward yourself.

Now, here's where things can get tricky.

Many of us, me included, have found food to be a primary reward.

Recently, I was talking with my husband, and he said, "We did a lot of good recently. My first thought is that you'd like to go to Cold Stone Creamery. My second thought is that you're staying away from carbohydrates and sugar."

I replied, "Go back to your first thought."

Develop a Menu of Rewards for Yourself

How could I reward myself with something *other than food?*

How about you? Think of the things you like to do, other than eating. Do you like to go to movies and enjoy the show with a diet soda? How about going to a museum?

Write in a journal or on a sheet of paper at least three things you could do to reward yourself for taking positive action.

Recently, I talked with my friend, Amanda.

"How are things going?" I asked.

Amanda paused for a moment. Then she got a big smile on her face. "I'm—I'm happy," she began. "I'm helping my sister revise her book. I like helping her bring something good into the world."

A significant number of people find that they experience a certain kind of reward—a great, happy feeling while helping another person. Here's the bonus: As you help another person, the God and Goddess also rejoice.

What about rewarding yourself with chocolate?

Recently, a friend asked, "What is your book about?"

I replied, "My book is a spiritual way of losing weight— and you can eat chocolate."

His eyes lit up with the last two words!

Everyone deserves to be rewarded for their positive actions. I know I want to be rewarded for staying with Goddess Style Weight Loss.

In the beginning of my journey with Goddess Style Weight Loss, I decided to "go easy on myself."

Yes, I cut out most processed foods and sugar.

Then I did something strategic. I allowed myself to eat dark chocolate. If you're careful, you can find a dark chocolate bar that has as little as 8 grams of sugar.

A square or two of dark chocolate a day can be beneficial to you. A study performed at Queen Margaret University suggests:

Eating dark chocolate (at least 70% cocoa) can do things such as:

- Improve your mood
- Stabilize your blood sugar
- Control your appetite
- Reduce your cravings for other foods

Dark chocolate reduces the digestion and absorption of fats and carbohydrates. This makes you feel full. It creates feelings of well-being and happiness.

Just look at dark chocolate as part of your *process of moderation.*

Dark chocolate still has:

Serving Size: 1.5 ounces

Calories: 220

Sugar: 12 grams

Sodium: 5 mg.

Fiber: 5 grams*

* article at ClevelandClinicWellness.com

So, I'm still inviting you to have a whole *Menu of Rewards for Yourself.*

Here are some of my non-food-related rewards:

- Walk where there are trees
- Talk with my "sister" (a really close friend)
- Talk with other close friends on the phone
- Hug my husband
- Watch a movie
- Watch TV shows, including *The Voice*
- Knit a project
- Enjoy taking photos
- Create jewelry
- Engage in digital illustration

What activities do you find to be intrinsically rewarding?

Section Eight:
Attract Something You Want #3

Finding Moments for God and Goddess

"I got nothing," my friend, Joe, said, as we were doing a comedy improvisation exercise.

"I got nothing" is the classic comment that a comedian says when he or she gets stuck and cannot add anything to a moment of improvisation.

Improvisation is on my mind because many of us, Wiccans, say that "we got nothing" in terms of "I don't have time to do a ritual. I'm busy!"

Does this sound familiar? I have the same problem in my life, too. Finding the time to do a whole ritual may not be practical every day or even once a week. There is a solution: You can "steal moments" of your day for the Gods and for your own sanity.

For example, I grabbed my husband and said a quick prayer to the Gods that we would land a client. Tonight, it's worked. The new person said, "Yes," and we have a new client.

Take a Moment and Light a Candle

Light a candle as a way to thank the Gods. I light offerings often to express my gratitude to the Gods for Their help.

Recite A Chant

Here's a chant:

Thank you Lord and Lady for today.
May all good things come my way.

This doesn't take long. Still, the effect can be profound. When you devote a moment to gratitude, it shifts your perception. Yes, you DO have things to be grateful for.

In summary, think of a quick prayer, lighting a candle or reciting a chant. These are some ways to "crowbar" in some time into your busy day.

It's worth it!

Section Eight:
Attract Something You Want #4

How to Make Your Own Goddess Style Weight Loss Sigil

Imagine putting a magical intention into an object to help with your *Goddess Style Weight Loss*. Why would you do that? Wiccans do this because they want the object to hold power to help them realize a personal desire. For example, you are starting Goddess Style, and you want the power of an object to help you—in this case, a sigil—to assist you in getting the results you want.

Making your own personal sigils can be easy. Some time ago, author/artist Austin Osman Spare devised a method for creating sigils.

Since that time, a number of authors have discussed Austin Osman Spare's process of making sigils. One book I appreciate is *Frater U. D.'s Practical Sigil Magic: Creating Personal Symbols for Success.*

I have made a couple of my own modifications to the

process.

First, throughout history, witches made sigils out of virgin parchment. But that is quite expensive. Also, if you're vegan and will not wear leather, you will want to use something else. Why? Parchment is typically made from goat skin. So, let's talk about a process devoid of parchment.

I use the heavier art paper, the kind that absorbs ink and which can be infused with different tinctures made with herbs. Water color paper is a nice choice, too.

What about inks? You could use one or of the many magickal inks on the market. My favorite is Dragons Blood Ink. But magickal inks can be expensive. So, you can make your own out of a high-grade ink such as Winsor Newton ink or India ink. To make it a magickal ink just add some essential oil to it, like myrrh. Mix and consecrate.

You can even use Sharpie pens as author Peter Paddon suggests. Just make sure to designate specific pens for only magickal work. They'll be part of your set of magickal tools.

You can use different colors for different desires. Here is a short list of colors and meanings that I include in my book *The Hidden Children of the Goddess:*

- Red: sex, desire, vitality, strength
- Orange: charm, confidence, joy, jealousy, persuasion
- Yellow: intellectual development, joy, intellectual strength
- Green: prosperity, abundance, fertility, money matters
- Blue: healing, protection, spiritual development
- Purple: the occult, power, magick
- Pink: love, friendship, compassion
- White: purity, innocence, peace, tranquility

Write out your desire on a scratch piece of paper; you can

use a single word or a phrase. Some examples are:

- I have an easy transition for my health at this time
- Happiness
- I let go of 30 lbs.
- Success

We'll now use the word "Success" as our example. Cross off all of the repeat letters in Success. You end up with S, U, C, and E. (You want only one of each letter that appears in the word.) Next, scramble the letters, getting S, E, U, and C (for example).

Now comes the fun part: Combine the letters together in an image.

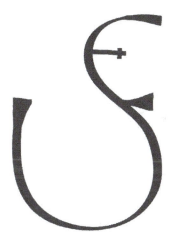

Can you find the letters?

With this process, you can make all sorts of sigils.

If you want to imbue it with a potion or tincture this is the time to do it. You can either soak the paper in your tincture or brush it on. Either way you must let it dry. Overnight is best.

Now with this new image (of combined letters), inscribe it

with your magical ink on your absorbent paper.

Now that you have the sigil, the next step is to breathe life into it with Pranic Breathing, also known as belly breathing. If you're familiar with yoga, you are probably familiar with Pranic Breathing techniques. Breathe in deeply; allow your stomach to inflate. Visualize pulling up energy from the earth. When you have built up enough energy in your lungs, blow it onto the sigil. This will charge it with your energy and further empower your intention.

Now place your sigil in a safe place and forget about it. Forgetting about it is the *toughest* part of the whole process. This helps the magick work.

As you can see, making your own sigils is quite easy and fun. After some practice, you will be able to do them quickly and easily.

Remember to consider using sigils to further your goals and get what you really want.

Sigils: Additional Techniques for Manifesting What You Want

Why would a Wiccan want to be adept with sigils? I've learned that sigils are a powerful way of manifesting what you want. I especially appreciate that sigils are useful for many purposes.

Five Ways You Can Use Sigils

Carve a Sigil on a Candle

When you carve a sigil on a candle, you're amplifying the power of standard candle magick.

Simply create your sigil, and then carve the sigil on your candle before you dress it. Complete the process by charging (you send energy through your hands to the candle) your candle.

Inscribe a Sigil on Jewelry

Many people inscribe a sigil onto jewelry that they wear. You can rotate your sigils by choosing to wear different pieces of jewelry on particular days. For example, if you want to express confidence on the day that you make a presentation at work, you could wear your jewelry inscribed with your confidence sigil.

Some Wiccans wear a specific sigil-inscribed jewelry piece for taking an exam. Some individuals wear their "workout at the gym" sigil to give them extra energy.

Create a Talisman

Wiccans enjoy talismans in that you can place them in a pocket where others cannot see them. Inscribe your sigil on virgin vellum or parchment paper. Additionally, you can place your talisman in a safe spot in your home where no one will disturb your magickal item.

Place the Sigil on Windows or Over Doors as Protection

Some Wiccans create a potion and use it to inscribe a sigil over a door or window. This form of sigil serves to guard your room or home. One can use lemon juice to inscribe a sigil—since lemon juice dries as invisible to the naked eye.

Get a Tattoo

Some Wiccans like to use henna (a form of temporary "tattoo"). Others get a permanent tattoo to stand for lifelong goals or devotions.

May you find your own way to use sigils to bless your life.

Section Nine
Create Abundance and
Your Own Confidence

If you're worried about paying your rent, how much energy do you have left for Goddess Style Weight Loss?

Have you talked with spiritual friends who are upside down in terms of their income?

A number of my Pagan friends talk about money and the people who have it in disparaging ways. Sometimes, it seems like they're holding onto some ideas from *other* spiritual paths.

Recently, a friend and I were talking about the Roman God, Bacchus, God of Mirth and Wine. He said, "How many people do you know who focus on mirth in their worship?"

Our conversation included Demeter, the Goddess of the Harvest. Her son is Plutus (this is related to *Ploutos*, literally "wealth" in the Greek language).

You may wonder why I'm including Plutus, God of Wealth, in this discussion. Did you know about Plutus? Do you think about increasing your abundance?

I've found that, at times in my life, I was stuck in pain so even the idea of "abundance" was *not* in my consciousness.

I'm inviting you to consider making your life full. Then you won't need food as "your only comfort."

Section Nine:
Create Abundance and Your Own Confidence #1

Getting Clients Spell

What you will need:

- 9 brown candles
- One gold candle
- 11 candle holders
- Attraction Oil
- Ritual tools

1. Cast Circle

Cleanse and consecrate the candles and oil. Dress the candles tip to base with Attraction Oil*. Place the gold candle in the middle of the altar's pentacle. Start in a spiral pattern placing nine brown candles around the gold one.

Light the gold candle first and say:

My golden honey as sweet as can be, attract clients like a swarm of happy bees to me.

* Attraction Oil includes: 3 drops Dragons Blood, 1 drop Cinnamon, 2 drops Basil Oil, and 1 drop Dill.

Light the first brown candle and say:

One little bee comes our way.

Light the next brown candle and continue with the other candles, while saying:

Soon another bee.... And another.... and another and another....comes my way.
Six.... Seven.... Eight.... Nine, little happy bees come my way.

Hold hands over the burning candles and say:

Who are these bees I may ask this day? Happy, well-matching clients willing to pay.

Say:

These bees are prosperous clients that are a good fit for me. May they find their way to me like insects drawn to a flame. May they flock to me like wild birds and gather like the roaming antelope across the great plains to me. Come one, come all, O-prosperous clients!
So mote it be!

2.   Do the Cakes and Wine Ceremony.
3.   Close the Circle.

* **Special Note:** When you do an abundance spell, do NOT talk about it for 24 hours. That's the way that you can guard the efficacy of your spell.

Section Nine:
Create Abundance and Your Own Confidence #2

The Wiccan's Solution for Doing What You Don't Feel Like Doing

Laundry! Paperwork! These are banes of my existence. (Okay, there are other difficult things, too …)

How can an exhausted Wiccan perk up and get difficult tasks done? (I'm talking about those tasks that we meet with procrastination!)

Candle Magic to Get You into Action

Light a red candle and say:

The red candle glows,
My energy grows.
My ease now flows.
Completing this task,
Will be fast.

I will be free at last.

May this process help you.

Section Nine:
Create Abundance and Your Own Confidence #3

Chant to Empower Talisman

Use this chant and a talisman for making your desires manifest.

Little talisman of mine,
Listen up, for it is time.

I empower you now, So, listen up!
For what I say must give me luck.

I call upon the powers of the Moon and Sun,
I call upon the powers of the Earth and Sky.

I call upon the four elements, Earth, Air, Fire, Water,
Give my talisman all your power.

I call upon the powers of the rivers and the seas,

Listen to my honest pleas.

May this talisman bring me _____ and luck,
Protect me from _____ and muck.

Lovely Lady of the Moon,
Give me this my greatest boon.

This boon or better by the end of the month.
So mote it be.

May this help you along your journey.

Section Nine:
Create Abundance and Your Own Confidence #4

What are the Most Important Things that Everyone Else Can Learn from Wiccans?

A reader asked me this question: "What are the most important things that everyone else can learn from Wiccans?"

Here are Five Wisdom-Points Wiccans Can Share with Others:

1) We value nature and the Earth as sacred.
Nature, as Wiccans see it, is a manifestation of Deity. Each flower and blade of grass has Deity inside them. All animals and people have the spirit of Deity within them. With this recognition, Wiccans view nature as sacred.

2) We recognize that men and women are equals.
In Wicca, no gender is considered better or greater than

another one. Women, in Wicca, hold clergy status. It's important to note that men are *not* looked down upon either. One of my friends said that he saw a website that noted how Wicca balances the polarities—the Goddess and the God.

3) We don't believe in Hell.

A number of Christian sects hold a belief in Hell. Wiccans note that they do *not* believe in the Christian Hell nor the "Christian Devil (evil one)."

(It's a hard to send someone to Hell when they don't believe in it. It's like telling a Christian to "Go to Mordor!")

When we enter a conversation about the belief in "sin," a number of details arise.

It's reported that numerous Christian sects believe that one can sin and therefore deserve to be placed in Christian Hell for eternity. Christian Hell is thought to be a place of eternal pain and suffering.

Thank goodness, Wiccan do *not* subscribe to such beliefs!

Wiccans do focus on The Three Times Law or Law of Three that guides our actions. The idea is: What you place into the universe returns to you three-fold. It seems smart to send out loving energy—and to receive three times the loving energy in return.

Wiccans also emphasize **The Wiccan Rede:** *Eight words the Wiccan Rede fulfill, An it harm none do what ye will.* Some think of the *Rede* as a law, but in fact, *Rede* means advice or counsel. What does this mean? It means that Wiccans do things that honor life. However, if one finds a deadly, venomous snake in the baby's room, a Wiccan might elect to send the snake to the Gods! The point is Wiccans are not pacifists. Wiccans do believe in self-defense.

4) We are responsible for our own actions.

When we make a choice whether good or bane, we own up to the consequences. (Wiccans do not say anything like "The devil made me do it.") We don't blame others for our mistakes. The outcomes of our choices are ours to reap. Therefore, Wiccans strive to only do good actions. Doing bad actions leads to suffering the bad whiplash of negative energy. Wiccans avoid that!

5) We are part of the God and Goddess; we are not separate from Deity.

Wiccans know that we are part of the God and Goddess. Women and men have both a feminine/Goddess side and a masculine/God side. We are never alone for the Gods are within us and around us at all times.

May these Wiccan insights be helpful to you.

Your Goddess Style Weight Loss Path Continues

As we complete this journey with this book, I celebrate your efforts and spiritual growth.

Please continue your path with me by viewing my articles at my blog at GoddessHasYourBack.com

Let's look at how far we have come. We have explored:

- Connect with God and Goddess
- Goddess Style Interactions with Food
- Release Yourself from the Need for Extra Weight to Feel Safe
- Be Smart about Having Energy
- Create Lots of Self-Care and Comfort (so food fades into the background)
- Protect Yourself
- Be Smart about Keeping Yourself Strong and Free of Energy-Drainers
- Attract Something You Want
- Create Abundance and Your Own Confidence

From this point forward, consider learning more about rituals, chants, tips, and ways to customize your rituals just for you ... and even more material when you sign up for my exclusive enewsletters. Just go to GoddessHasYourBack.com and click on the link (on the right side of the webpage).

Consider my previous six books. Thank you.

Blessed Be,
Moonwater SilverClaw

Get Real Support. Take the 5-Week Online Course:

ABOUT THE AUTHOR

Moonwater SilverClaw is a Wiccan High Priestess and member of the Covenant of the Goddess and the New Wiccan Church. She has trained people new to Wicca. Her personal story reveals how Wicca saved her life and helped her strengthen herself to secure her release from an abusive marriage.

Moonwater has been practicing Wicca since 1990, first as a solitary and then in a coven.

Moonwater posts at her blog,

GoddessHasYourBack.com

[with visitors from 178 countries]

She felt called to write the blog and write 7 books even though she is dyslexic. She works with a team of editors. She says, "I wish to educate those who don't understand what the Craft is about. Some people may not yet identify themselves as Pagan, but they'd like more information."

Moonwater has addressed college students in Comparative Religion classes for over ten years. She leads workshops. She lives with her cat Magick and her sweetheart of many years; he is one of her editors. She enjoys knitting and photography.

Her work is endorsed by Wiccan notables including Patrick McCollum (receiver of the Mahatma Gandhi Award for the Advancement of Religious Pluralism).

Moonwater SilverClaw can be contacted at:

AskAWitchNow@gmail.com

Or at her blog:

GoddessHasYourBack.com

Special Offer Just for Readers of this Book:

Contact Moonwater SilverClaw at askawitchnow@gmail.com for special discounts on books, consulting, workshops and presentations. Just mention your experience with this book.

Excerpt from

Goddess Has Your Back

by Moonwater SilverClaw

CHAPTER 1:
GODDESS HAS YOUR BACK

Would you like your Wiccan path to lift up your self-esteem?

Would you simply like to feel better?

This book helps you actually feel your connection with

the Goddess on a daily basis—even moment to moment.

As I mentioned in my first two books, *The Hidden Children of the Goddess* and *Beyond the Law of Attraction to Real Magick,* Wicca saved my life and empowered me to leave an abusive marriage.

As a High Priestess, I have supported friends, family, and colleagues in times of need. My blog GoddessHasYourBack.com gives me a weekly opportunity to support website visitors from over 178 countries.

This book gives *us* the space and time to really explore magickal practices, rituals, meditations and experiences that you'll find comforting and uplifting.

My journey upon this path began with meeting the Gods. The Gods showed me the true path to self love and acceptance. Where I saw nothingness and unworthiness, they showed me abundance and a unique specialness that I had.

Now I will let you in on a secret. *You have your own unique specialness that no one else has.* It is yours, and yours alone. This new path is yours to discover and walk. Just like my own path, your path is a beautiful discovery simply waiting for you. Prepare to step forward on this new, wondrous, and beautiful path.

Let's take the next step.

Secret of How to Do Magick

When I first started doing magick it was really hit or miss, most often *mess.* My spell work was just not as effective as I wanted it to be. What was I doing wrong?

If you have wondered the same thing, you have probably done similar mistakes. For example, I'd do a money spell, but I'd just get new problems!

The real problem was, like many people, I just wanted a

big payday. What I didn't know was that this is really the wrong way to approach a lack of money.

Many, if not most, spells written today are focused on the external opportunities or even requesting gifts from the Gods. Focusing on just the external can create new problems.

What if I could tell you a **Secret of how to do magick**—in a way where you avoid ethics issues about money?

I have mentored a number of people about this *Secret.* Now I will share with you this Secret.

A phrase from the poem by Doreen Valiente entitled *The Charge of the Goddess* tells us how to do magick well. But many of us, like my younger self, just don't see it. The line I'm talking about is: "...if that which thou seekest thou findest not within thee, thou wilt never find it without thee."

This line invites us to look within as we approach our magickal work.

Instead of focusing on how to get money from outside sources, focus within. How? Instead of asking for a handout from the universe, ask, **"How I can create more energy in myself to obtain my desire? How can I make myself open to more prosperity?"**

Let's get more specific. ...

END OF EXCERPT from the book *Goddess Has Your Back* Available from top online retailers.

* * * * * *

Read an excerpt from *Beyond the Law of Attraction to Real Magick* – on the next page.

Excerpt from

Beyond the Law of Attraction to Real Magick
How You Can Remove Blocks to Prosperity, Happiness and Inner Peace

by Moonwater SilverClaw

Self-perspective: Overcome the Blockage of Not Feeling Worthy

Do you feel worthy of the best that life has to offer? Maybe on the conscious level you say, "Sure. Bring it on. The new house, new car, and a real, loving relationship."

But have you ever sabotaged your chances of getting exactly what you wanted?

Self-sabotage can occur because of feeling not worthy on a subconscious level.

If it's subconscious, how can we deal with this?

Good question.

Soon I will share with you a Self-Love Meditation.

But first let's talk about magick. The whole premise of this book is that there is a way to go about the Law of Attraction with more power.

To put it simply, the Law of Attraction is a form of magick, but people who read an introductory book on the Law of Attraction are often denied enough information to truly make the Law of Attraction work in their own lives.

So, to really make a positive difference in your life, we need to talk about real magick. I spell magick with a "k" to distinguish it from stage magic you see on television.

Magick is a natural power, *not* a supernatural one. Who uses magick? In my spiritual path, Wicca, one is trained to use magick in appropriate ways.

When Wiccans do magick, they channel *natural* energies and create change with them.

Well, if Wicca isn't really supernatural then why practice Wicca at all?

To put it simply, *you want something.* That's probably why you were interested in the Law of Attraction in the first place. Now in the context of learning real magick, you'll be able to fully use the Law of Attraction. And that's good news!

Everyone is different and has their own answer to that question. I like to think of religion as a bottle of wine. Let's say you have three different people who all taste the same bottle of wine. The first person points out that the flavor has accents of oak. The second praises the hints of apple in it, and the third enjoys the floral notes. They are all right. The wine contains all the flavors they described. But each person detected something different. Religion is like that. Deity can't be entirely known. So, the truth of it is scattered into many faiths.

In Wicca, we honor the God and the Goddess. If that's new to you, you can substitute the label of Higher Power or God or Deity.

The Gods and Goddesses have helped me and they can help you, too. The first thing they taught me was self-love.

Before we go further, let's make a distinction between self-love and self-conceit (or being stuck in one's ego).

Self-love is about kindness and support. So, it's a good thing. It is NOT about your ego or puffing yourself up.

Let me show you how the Gods changed my perspective on myself for the better.

One of the best exercises I learned is meditation. Through reflective meditation, the Gods helped me understand how skewed my perception of myself really was. This was a key turning point for me.

One thing you always hear about are affirmations, but for many of us these just don't work.

First, let's cover what an affirmation is. It's a personal, positive statement. It can be as simple as "I feel terrific" or "I make a lot of money."

For many, the above statements don't work. Why?

A number of people have said, "It just sounds like I'm lying to myself."

Like myself, many people's inner self-beliefs interfere with these positive statements. For an example, if I used the affirmation "I am thin," my brain would object with "No, I'm not. Look in the mirror." It's not true. No matter how hard you try to pound that new idea into your brain, your brain pounds just as hard back.

So how did the Gods help me deal with this problem? They inspired me to create a Self-Love Meditation.

So instead of the uphill battle of an affirmation, we'll use the Self-Love Meditation to work with the situation.

END OF EXCERPT from *Beyond the Law of Attraction to Real Magick*

Purchase your copy of the above books (paperback or ebook) at top online retailers.

See **Free Chapters** of *Moonwater SilverClaw's 7 books* at a top online retailer – including *Be A Wiccan Badass.*

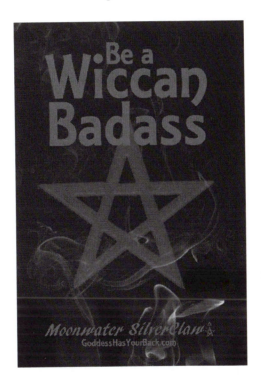

Made in the USA
Middletown, DE
10 November 2020